Dr. James Mullin
was the father of Gladys (Aunt).
She was one of the first women to go to
University in Cardiff in the 1890's and
then she married John Arthur Clark
                                    forgotten
They had 7 children. He was
a brother of Gladys Theresa Clark,
later Mitchell when she married
George Herbert.

CLASSICS OF IRISH HISTORY
General Editor: Tom Garvin

Other titles in this series:

P. S. O'Hegarty
The Victory of Sinn Féin
with an Introduction by Tom Garvin
(1998)

Walter McDonald
Some Ethical Questions of Peace and War
with an Introduction by Tom Garvin
(1998)

Joseph Johnston
Civil War in Ulster
edited by Roy Johnston
(1999)

THE STORY OF A TOILER'S LIFE

James Mullin

edited by
Patrick Maume

"O socii (neque enim ignari sumus ante malorum)
O passi graviora: dabit Deus his quoque finem."
—*Virgil, Aeneidos Lib. I*

University College Dublin Press
Preas Choláiste Ollscoile Bhaile Átha Cliath

First published by Maunsel & Roberts, 1921

This edition first published by
University College Dublin Press, 2000
Introduction © Patrick Maume 2000

ISBN 1 900621 40 1
ISSN 1393–6883

University College Dublin Press
Newman House, 86 St Stephen's Green, Dublin 2, Ireland
www.ucdpress.ie

Cataloguing in Publication data
available from the British Library

Introduction typeset in Ireland in Baskerville
by Elaine Shiels, Bantry, Co. Cork
Printed in Ireland by Colour Books, Dublin

CONTENTS

Introduction by Patrick Maume

INTRODUCTION
Patrick Maume

James Mullin
Biographical Note

James Mullin was born in Cookstown in 1846, the only son of labouring parents who rented a two-roomed cottage with a pigsty and half a rood of garden. His father died before James was old enough to remember him, and his mother supported them by field labour in the summer and autumn, outworking for the local textile mill in the winter, and subletting the pigsty and one room of the cabin. At one point a pig shared their own room. Mullin's mother was literate and endowed her son with a desire for knowledge and a burning self-respect. He received his basic education at three schools—one, which a few years earlier might have been called a "hedge school" was run by an elderly master in his own house and terminated with the master's death; the second was a Church of Ireland infant school, and the third was a national school which, although managed by a Catholic priest, had not developed the religious and sexual segregation which were soon to dominate the Irish educational system. He left school at the age of eleven and became a labourer; after being dismissed by the local landlord for reading while on duty and being exploited by his paternal uncle, he apprenticed himself as an unskilled carpenter and wheelwright. At the same time he read every book he could borrow from neighbours or acquire from travelling book-pedlars. He wished to become a poet and published verse in a local newspaper; he was annoyed to find this regarded as a sign of eccentricity.

Mullin's relations with Orangemen whom he met during his labours were surprisingly friendly when it is remembered that Cookstown, lying on the ethnic border and with a slight Protestant majority, was a noted centre of Orangeism and Fenianism, Mullin himself being a Fenian. An uncle who lived in Dungannon had served a term of imprisonment for killing a member of the Orange lodge known as the "Killymoon Wreckers" during a party fight. East Tyrone's Orange traditions go back to the participation of Tyrone Orangemen at the "Battle of the Diamond" in 1795, which led to the foundation of the Order. (It was an earlier generation of "Wreckers" who raided the Carleton household near Clogher during the novelist William Carleton's childhood; more recently, the Killyman district near Dungannon, a centre of Orange violence in the 1790s, produced Joel Patton, leader of the hardline Spirit of Drumcree group.) Mullin's experiences may reflect recognition by the Orangemen that he was an eccentric partly estranged from his own community (though he made it a point of honour to insist on observing Catholic duties while in Orange company), as well as his willingness to help illiterate Orangemen with paperwork. It should be remembered that Mullin encountered the order at a time when the role as a semi-tolerated paramilitary adjunct to state power which it enjoyed earlier in the nineteenth century had largely fallen into disuse, and before the Home Rule crisis transformed it from a largely plebeian body under aristocratic leadership into a more "respectable" organisation serving as the backbone of the Unionist political machine and patronage organisation. In later life Mullin objected to those who spoke insultingly of Orangemen, and his memoir repeatedly insists on the importance of reconciling Orange and Green. His nationalism was combined with a sense of identity as a Northerner, and he even displays a certain fellow-feeling for Scots. (He admired Burns's poems, though not his pretentious *Letters to Clarinda*, and the fact that Mullin was mistaken for a Scot when travelling in Scotland suggests that he retained his Northern accent.)

Mullin's earliest reading included popular nationalist literature; an old copy of Paine's *Rights of Man* made him a lifelong republican, an attitude encouraged by his mother's stories of a relative's sufferings in 1798 and her insistence on pride and self-reliance. Mullin joined the Fenian Brotherhood in 1865, participated in their drilling in the Sperrin Mountains, and contributed verse to their papers, *The Irish People* and *The Irishman*. For a time he acted as the papers' local agent, and was disappointed to escape arrest. His account of the Fenians emphasises their conflict with the Catholic clergy at local and national level.[1] In retrospect he thought some of the clergy's concerns about the movement had been well founded but that their bullying manner and insistence on unconditional obedience provoked justifiable resistance; he maintained that the Fenians' defiance paved the way for Ireland's subsequent political gains, and despite changing views he remained proud to have been a Fenian.

Mullin himself had lost his religious faith through bitterness at the inability of prayer to remedy hunger, and exasperation at the inability of the numerous religious controversialists whom he read to produce definitive proof of their arguments, but he conformed outwardly from respect for his mother and unwillingness to seem to desert "his side" in a divided community. He criticised the tendency for belief in Heaven to act as a "spiritual opiate" dulling rebellion against this-wordly suffering, but he also emphasises both his mother's piety (which did not prevent her from sending him to a Protestant school, encouraging his Fenianism, and helping him to attend a Queen's College despite pulpit denunciations) and her "rare capacity for squarely facing bare and brutal realities and never replacing them with flattering illusions". In later life Mullin professed a Victorian agnosticism which saw the value of Christianity as lying in its ethical teaching and its supernatural elements as myths which deserved some respect for sustaining those who had not advanced far enough to do without them.

By various means Mullin had continued to acquire knowledge, teaching himself Latin and Greek and gaining admittance to the local library and debating society. After quarrelling with his employer he went to Magherafelt in search of work while continuing to support his mother; unknown to him she saved most of the money he sent her, despite her own age, ill-health, and want, and then suggested to him that he should try to enrol at the local secondary school, Cookstown Academy, in order to advance his education. The sight of a working man with intellectual interests attracted interest and sympathy from the headmaster, J.G. Houston, who encouraged him and eventually persuaded him to study for a scholarship to Queen's College Galway. (The Queen's Colleges had been severely affected by the Catholic hierarchy's condemnation; hence the relative weakness of competition.)

With some help from friends, labouring work during the summer, and terrible sacrifices by his mother, Mullin was able to establish himself at the College in 1871, and when his mother died shortly after he received his BA he sold the tenant-right of their holding and left Cookstown for ever. He supported himself by scholarships, tutoring and journalism while working for a medical qualifications; though better nourished and speaking with respect of the professors (including Thomas Maguire, later notorious for his connection with the Pigott forgeries), he was always acutely aware of the need for incessant hard work and the danger of drifting into the self-indulgent life of a perpetual student.[2] Queen's College medical degrees were not as highly regarded as those awarded by the Dublin medical schools (some of which Mullin obtained at a later stage in his career), and did not qualify their holder for many of the available medical jobs in Ireland. Hence on his final graduation in 1880, Mullin emigrated to Britain.

After the failure of Fenianism, Mullin had abandoned politics as futile and regarded all politicians as self-serving windbags (a view shared by his Fenian and Orange friends), but he was shocked back into action by the wave of anti-Irish prejudice which swept through Britain as a result of the Land War and the Phoenix Park murders. Mullin had abandoned Catholic observance but insisted on describing himself as an Irish Roman Catholic to prospective employers, although he knew it would prejudice them against him, because his self-respect would not let him seem to abandon his mother's religion for his own advantage. After some years' work as a locum Mullin married and set up a successful medical practice in Cardiff, where he became active in the Irish National League and was made chairman of the local branch.

As a local activist he met leading nationalists who visited Cardiff. He revered Michael Davitt, whose life and opinions in some ways resembled his own, but his impression of Charles Stewart Parnell was very unfavourable, and when the Split came, Mullin, like Davitt, opposed Parnell as an arrogant autocrat whose selfish egotism was playing into the hands of Ireland's enemies. (In retrospect, the old man was more impressed by Parnell's greatness and thought he should have supported him.) Pearse, whom Mullin met at the 1899 Cardiff Pan-Celtic Conference, seemed "unable to differentiate between facts and fancies". (Pearse was very young and Mullin may have been influenced by a recent quarrel with the Gaelic League over his own publicly expressed view that the need for children to learn a trade should take precedence over the teaching of Irish.) Mullin's vignettes of the leading figures whom he met are valuable though hardly comprehensive (he records the magnanimity which was an important part of Davitt's character, but not the bitterness which inspired some of his more scurrilous speeches during the Parnell Split); it says much about the obscurity into which *The Story of a Toiler's Life* has fallen that it went unused by biographers.

Mullin retired from his medical practice in 1908 after developing diabetes, but rather than accept a passive life of invalidism he embarked on a series of sea voyages, whose cost he subsidised by acting as ships' doctor and by writing accounts of his experiences for newspapers. These voyages were ended by the outbreak of the First World War. In his last years Mullin wrote an autobiography, *The Story of a Toiler's Life*; from internal evidence he seems to have begun it in 1915 and finished it in 1917. Lacking belief in an afterlife, he wrote to make sense of his life and leave some memorial to future generations. He died early in 1920;[3] the book was published by Maunsel and Roberts in 1921.

The Story of a Toiler's Life

Mullin's principal models were William Carleton's autobiography[4] and the picaresque stories of Charles Lever, but
while Carleton's book is recognisably the product of an oral
and discursive tradition and Lever sent his adventurers from
one escapade to another with only the most rudimentary
structure and perfunctory endings, Mullin's book (despite
some anecdotal digressions) is novel-like in his tight focus on
his own life and thoughts. While Mullin shows himself
anxious to acknowledge all those who helped him, he generally
does not give the names of his acquaintances who were not
already public figures, not even his mother. (His marriage,
which he describes as happy, is barely touched upon; presum-
ably he saw it as private.) Some allusions, easily understood by
contemporaries, need explanation. The graduate Mullin
attacked for denouncing Queen's College Galway was the
future Home Rule MP Frank Hugh O'Donnell, a fantasist
whose variegated career was held together by a delusional self-
image as the dispossessed descendant of idealised Gaelic
Catholic aristocrats; at different times this led him to attack
the Queen's Colleges as an Ultramontane and defend them as
a Gallican.[5] Mullin's medical acquaintance who organised
Rossa's lecture tour (in 1895–6) was Dr Mark Ryan, the
prominent London Fenian. Sir E.J. Reed (Liberal MP for
Pembroke 1874–80, Cardiff City 1880–95 and 1900–5) was a
shipowner notoriously unenthusiastic about Home Rule, who
eventually defected to the Liberal Unionists in support of
Tariff Reform. The one British newspaper which Mullin, at
the time of the First World War, saw as maintaining the anti-
Irish prejudice which the British press as a whole displayed
after the Phoenix Park murders was the Tory Diehard *Morning
Post* (which came to see the IRA as a Judaeo-Bolshevik con-
spiracy, and merged with the *Daily Telegraph* in the 1930s).

Mullin was a reader not a storyteller, and the book gives
fascinating glimpses of the residual awe surrounding literacy in
a semi-literate (almost pre-literate) society where an assiduous
reader might be revered as a saint, on the assumption that all

texts were religious, or suspected of being a disciple of "Harry Stotle or Cornelyus the Grupper" (i.e. Aristotle and the alchemist Cornelius Agrippa, portrayed in popular tradition as powerful magicians).[6] The same awe lies behind Carleton's depiction of hedge-schoolmasters using ostentatious pedantry to impress their audiences; but while Mullin recognised Carleton's world, the society in which he lived was changing rapidly. The labouring class from which he came, always poor, was in post-Famine decline. The depth of the poverty which formed the background to Mullin's early years is easily overlooked because it is only disclosed in casual references, with the experiences of years passed over in a few sentences: the remark that the landlord, who after the Famine bought the estate on which the Mullins lived, surrounded his Big House with "many acres of land levelled from the fields of his former tenants"; the cast-off clothes brought over from the Glasgow slums by pedlars for sale to the Irish poor; the ever-present fear of typhus; the workdays extending for twelve hours or more; the precision with which he recalls small sums of money paid 40 or 50 years previously; the fact that only after receiving his scholarship and settling in Galway did he consider himself adequately fed and free from hunger; the retired Cardiff doctor waking on Monday mornings with the boy labourer's sense of dread and gloom and comparing his own childhood with the carefree play of his grandchildren.

Not all of these post-Carletonian changes were for the worse. While Mullin's tramp from Cookstown to Magherafelt in search of work, sleeping in a doss-house during the week and walking eight miles back to his mother at weekends, might have come out of Carleton, his ability to undertake long journeys by rail marks a significant change since Carleton's time. (At a crucial moment in his career, having found a pound note in the marketplace, he went to Belfast for the day to buy classical texts.) Carleton's only route to higher education lay through Maynooth; Mullin gained access to the Queen's Colleges through a mixture of luck, hard work, and his mother's self-sacrifice.

The Queen's Colleges were intended to create a Catholic professional class which would work the Union, and it is easy to see Mullin as a radical tamed by the system. This view, however, would be over-simplistic; his book is the story of a quest for self-respect as much as for knowledge and economic security. The answer lies in an aspect of the Irish Party which is often ignored. In Irish history the Party is seen as a purely conservative and "obesely bourgeois" body, but it also contained many professionals of uncertain social status, drawn from urban communities in Britain and Ireland. (The Party's MPs contained a disproportionate number of London journalists who could support themselves at Westminster before MPs were paid salaries.) The idea that such a class, exempt from provincial constraints, might discard Catholic belief and clerical authority was one of the elements that complicated Party relations with the Catholic hierarchy. (It did not help that British radical papers sympathetic to Home Rule, like *Reynolds' News*, also tended to publish secularist polemics and suggestive stories and were regularly denounced and destroyed by protesters in Ireland.) Some of these radicals were indeed, as their critics saw them, adventurers and opportunists; others genuinely saw the Irish cause as part of a pan-British progressive struggle.

In his later career Mullin's hero Davitt argued that Ireland's wrongs could be resolved by uniting with the "British democracy" represented by the Radical wing of the Liberal Party in seeing Home Rule as part of a shared agenda of social reform to be obtained by overcoming the common enemy—the privileged elite represented by the Conservative Party. Such a view made it possible for those like Mullin to see Home Rule as the culmination of the tradition of 1798 and Fenianism, rather than compromising it. It also accorded well with Mullin's experience of raising himself from poverty within the structures of the British state, and by the time of the First World War the erstwhile Fenian was writing of "our Empire" and uncritically echoing anti-German propaganda. Despite this acculturation Mullin retained some of his radical attitudes (in discussing Pearse's execution he implies opposition to capital punishment as such).

After the fall of Parnell and the retirement of Gladstone the concept of an alliance with the "British Democracy" came under increasing criticism, not only because many Liberals like Sir E.J. Reed saw Home Rule as a political liability, but also because of chronic tensions between Liberal attitudes on social, religious and economic matters and those which prevailed in Ireland. These tensions were exacerbated by the rise of a new generation of separatists and cultural nationalists, who emphasised those factors which distinguished Ireland from Britain and the increasing authority and confidence of the Irish Catholic Church. Some of the conflicts between the Irish Party organisation in Britain and the Catholic clergy, which affected Mullin's later political career, reflected the fact that the clergy preferred their parishioners to support the Conservatives, who favoured state support for denominational education, while the Irish Party's Liberal allies were fiercely hostile to church schools.[7]

For post-Parnellite separatists like Arthur Griffith the project of a "Union of Hearts" with the British Democracy represented national apostasy and self-delusion. Mullin shows how it could be seen as an honourable project which delivered concrete benefits despite its ultimate failure. By the time the book appeared, the Home Rule political project had been decisively defeated and the new Irish state was to be shaped by his clericalist and Gaelic Revival opponents. In these changed circumstances *The Story of a Toiler's Life* passed almost unnoticed, but it is of lasting value not only to historians of Irish literacy and education, religious belief and unbelief, and nineteenth-century nationalism, but to anyone who appreciates this powerful human document of a struggle with the physical and intellectual hunger of post-Famine Ireland.[8]

Notes

1 For the wider context to this conflict see Oliver Rafferty, *The Church, the state and the Fenian threat 1861–75* (Basingstoke, 1999).

2 Tadhg Foley (ed.), *From Queen's College to National University: Essays on the Academic History of QCG/UCG/NUI, Galway* (Dublin, 1999) describes the working of the nineteenth-century college and outlines the careers and personalities of staff members mentioned by Mullin. His matriculation and graduation dates are given on p. 145.

3 *Freeman's Journal*, 5 January 1920, p. 5.

4 William Carleton, *Autobiography* (Dublin, 1896 as vol.1 of D.J. O'Donoghue, *Life of William Carleton*—reprinted several times, most recently in 1997).

5 Frank Hugh O'Donnell, *Mixed education in Ireland* (London, 1870) was the work that provoked Mullin's outrage. O'Donnell's later views are expressed in *The ruin of education in Ireland* (London, 1902) and *Paraguay on Shannon: the price of a political priesthood* (London, 1908).

6 Angela Bourke, *The Burning of Bridget Cleary* (London, 1999) gives an interesting analysis of the role and persistence of folk-beliefs in nineteenth-century rural Ireland.

7 Patrick Maume *The Long Gestation: Irish nationalist political life 1891–1918* (Dublin, 1999).

8 Those seeking further discussion of Mullin should consult Patrick Maume "James Mullin, the poor scholar; a self-made man from Carleton's country", *Irish Studies Review*, vii (1999), pp. 29–39, Paul O'Leary's forthcoming history of the Irish in Wales will give further information on the context of Mullin's later career.

NOTE ON THE TEXT

The text of this edition of *The Story of a Toiler's Life* is printed
as a facsimile of the original book published by Maunsel &
Roberts (Dublin and London) 1921

THE STORY OF A TOILER'S LIFE

CHAPTER I

A HARD CHILDHOOD

I was born in Cookstown, County Tyrone, Ireland, in 1846, when the shadow of the great Famine was gathering unseen, but had not yet fallen on the devoted country ; wherein he who was born poor died poor, after a life of slavery and semi-starvation, submissively borne in the fond hope of a glorious compensation hereafter—that spiritual opiate which deadens " divine discontent," reconciles the wretch to his wretchedness, paralyses his efforts to rise against it, and safeguards the power of the oppressor.

My parents were working people—a fact I might boast of had they been of my own choosing, for as such they belonged to the most valuable section of the world's inhabitants. In my boyhood days, when, like all boys, I knew everything, I traced my family back to Heremon, the Milesian prince who, with his brother Heber, landed in Ireland on Thursday, 1st May, *anno mundi* 2984 ; a date so circumstantial must defy contradiction, even though the hour of the day is not mentioned.

I learned from an aunt who was a good Irish scholar that the English equivalent for my name was

B

Miller, which was assumed by some of our name-sakes, who had risen in the world, to prove their pure Anglo-Saxon origin. I always thanked Heaven that none of my forebears ever soared so high on borrowed wings.

It was not an entirely unknown occurrence in the dark days of Landlord and Church ascendancy for some Irish families to change their names and religion in order to curry favour with the party who dominated their destiny. I knew several such families in our neighbourhood, and in justice to them I must say they did not dishonour the name they assumed by showing bigotry against the names they left.

I was an only child, and my father died when I was too young to remember him. After his funeral, my mother, as she afterwards told me, started her widowhood with the possession of fourpence, which she spent on soap for a general washing-up.

But if she was left hopelessly destitute of worldly means, she had a stout heart and willing hands, and a rare capacity for squarely facing bare and brutal realities, and never replacing them with flattering illusions, or, as she herself said, never mistaking a shilling for a sovereign. So she at once turned to the first work that offered itself, and this was field labour, at which, whether in the hay or harvest-field, she proved equal to any other worker, even of that sex which is called the stronger ; nay, I have even known her to get extra pay for taking the lead in a gang of reapers. Work of this sort was, however, only obtainable during the summer months, and even then only when the weather was fine. In the winter months she used to spin flax and wind thread on reels for the use of the weaving factory. Her pay for work in the fields varied from sixpence to eightpence per day of twelve hours, with half-an-hour's rest for breakfast and a full hour for dinner. At six p.m. the day's work ended, and as she returned from the fields, usually carrying an armful of brambles for firewood, I well remember running forth to meet and welcome her with a kiss, and I still look back on those meetings as the happiest moments of my life.

Poor as we were, we were not so poor as our neighbours, for we owned the house we lived in, and in which I was born. It still stands, with a hawthorn bush in front of it planted by the hands of my mother.

It was built, or rather rebuilt, when my mother got married, and her small dowry was invested in it under conditions which go to prove that my father was no better as a business man than his son is reputed to be. The site of the house was a tumble-down cabin, whose occupants sold the goodwill thereof according to what was known as the Ulster Custom. The ground landlord was never consulted in the matter, and probably knew nothing about it till my father applied to have his name put on the rent roll. This raised no difficulty, and I am not sure whether it raised the rent, which was fifty shillings a year. But the landlord, like the tenant, was a happy-go-lucky being, and during the four remaining years of my father's life no rent was asked for and none was paid. My mother, in the first year of her widowhood, was reminded of this unpleasant fact, when a new landlord purchased the property, and gave her notice to pay these arrears under penalty of eviction. She approached " his honour," and induced him to come to a settlement by promising to pay off the debt in half-yearly instalments of one pound—a promise which she faithfully fulfilled.

But until it was fulfilled she was served with a notice to quit each half-year, so that if the instalment was not forthcoming she might be evicted without that loss of time which serving another notice would entail. Yet hers the house remained until her death, when I sold it, or perhaps I should say the goodwill of it, for twenty-two pounds to pay the expenses of the funeral.

Attached to the house was half-a-rood of garden, a providential means of supplying us with enough potatoes to tide over the winter.

The house was a thatched cottage divided into a room and kitchen, both of the same dimensions. We lived in the kitchen, and let the room to a family at tenpence a week.

There was also a pigstye, or, as we called it, a " pigscrew," which we let to another family at sixpence a week. This abode had, of course, neither window nor chimney, the smoke escaping through a hole in the roof, and the light entering through the open doorway. In fine weather the family took their meals on a patch of grass in front and seemed quite happy in their surroundings. The father was a rag and bone collector, and their name was Williamson.

Being of Anglo-Saxon origin, as Froude, the purveyor of race prejudice, would proudly point out, they prospered so well that they ultimately moved into another mansion, for which they could not have paid less than fifteen pence per week.

The next tenant for the same residence was a Mrs. McFarlane, who by-and-bye turned it into a stye for human swine, which necessitated her eviction, and I well remember my mother throwing her things out. It then rose to its original status, and for some years housed a pig, but, ultimately falling out of repair, obliged us to transfer its inmate to our kitchen. My objections to this were met with the reply that all dirt was removable except moral dirt, and that it was far cleaner to live with a pig in the corner than to live in comfort at the expense of other people.

Owing to the fact that we owned a house and garden, and drew a weekly rental from our room, we were considered well-to-do people amongst our neighbours, who were only cottiers at a rental of one shilling a week. My mother always kept up the dignity of a property-owner, and all through the year of the Famine, though our need was as great as our neighbours, when soup and Indian meal were being distributed amongst them, she never allowed such relief to enter our house.

I cannot say that I have any personal recollections of the Famine, but I heard many harrowing stories of corpses being found by the wayside with their mouths stained green from attempting to eat grass and various weeds. And many a time I have seen mothers spread their Indian meal porridge over the platter, so that it would cover as large a surface as possible and flatter the eyes of the children while it deceived their stomachs. Our great novelist, Carleton, describes the same trick in *The Black Prophet* ; and, indeed, it can be seen to-day in any of our cheap restaurants where the customer's plate is covered with slices of meat as thin as tissue paper. In those dark days I was frequently treated in this way, and, if I complained, would be told to pray over the pittance and then I should find it satisfying. But as often as I did so, I was not satisfied, till at last I looked upon the good advice as a piece of grim irony.

No person who did not live amongst the poor in Ireland in my young days can realise what poverty is. The staple food was potatoes—potatoes morning, noon, and night, unvarying as the rising and setting of the sun, for breakfast, dinner, and supper, washed down with mouthfuls of sour buttermilk, or flavoured with a pinch of salt. How well I remember the tubers, boiled " in their jackets," being emptied from the black pot into the shallow circular basket. Around this the eaters used to sit on stools, or any-how they could, and each grabbing a tuber from the side nearest to him, would scratch off the skin with his nails, and accompany each bite with a mouthful of the buttermilk.

I was not only unable to feast in that fashion, but was almost unable to see others do so, and consequently was considered a degenerate creature who would never develop any strength of body or mind. Be that as it may, I developed an aversion to the potato which I have never been able to overcome, and this not only on personal, but on national grounds. I con-sider it has been a curse to Ireland by lowering the standard of living almost to the brute level and making the poor people content with that wretched lot. Furthermore, it tended to atrophy of the brain, and distension of the intestines, because it required little industry and less ingenuity to produce ; and because it required to be eaten in enormous quantities before it yielded sufficient proteid matter for the production of vital energy. This fact was often pointed out to us students in those " subjects " in the dissecting room whose food in life had been " the national tuber."

A favourite article of food in Tyrone, especially on Sundays, was nettle broth. With a sprinkling of

barley, and if possible a small bit of lard or dripping,
and, when we could afford it, an oatmeal dumpling,
we had in this a treat and no mistake.   Mention of
this treat reminds me of the following story, which
in my young days was very popular at our firesides.
A poor woman, the mother of a half-witted son,
bought a sheep's head in our Saturday market, intending a grand spread for the Sunday dinner.   So
next day she made two oatmeal dumplings, got a
quantity of nettle tops and a handful of barley, and
putting these and the sheep's head into her big pot
for a nice sup of broth, set the whole over the fire to
get boiled against her return from church, leaving
her son in charge with strict injunctions to see that
it was properly attended to and not allowed to boil
over.   Deeply impressed with the importance of his
duty, the lad every few minutes kept lifting the lid
off the pot to make sure that the contents were all
right.   Having done this quite a number of times he
suddenly found that one of the dumplings had disappeared, while the other was gyrating on the surface
with the sheep's head close behind it.   Smelling
danger, he at once ran at top speed to the church,
where a large congregation was listening to a highly
edifying sermon.   Catching his mother's eye as soon
as he entered, he bawled out at the top of his voice :
" Come home, mother, come home as fast as the divil
can dhrive ye, for the sheep's head has ait wan av
the dumplin's, an' it's chasin' the other all roun' the
pot."
   If we saw less of the Famine than the poor people
of the south and west, we saw a great deal of its
aftermath in typhus, or, as we called it, " the spotted
fever."   It spread amongst our neighbours to an
alarming extent.   Whole families were laid up with

it, and few of them recovered without the loss of at
least one member. How any of them escaped seems
a miracle possible for Providence only to have worked.
Their mode of living outraged all the laws of health.
Many of their dwellings consisted of one apartment
only, and hardly any of more than two. Some of
them lodged a pig both day and night in the corner,
and in others the hens roosted on poles swung
horizontally from the rafters. One small window, or
at most two, impossible to open, admitted the light.
and the dunghill was close to the door—the front
door in country houses, the back door in town houses.
The water was obtained from a well in the garden,
and sometimes from an adjacent brook. In my own
town there was not a pump.

It is not to be wondered at that a half-starved
people living under such conditions should suffer so
many losses—the wonder is that any of them should
survive. That they did so was, in my opinion, due
to the fact that their days were spent in the open
air, both men and women being field labourers.

No guidance was necessary to point out a house
wherein the fever raged ; that fact was revealed by
the acrid stench issuing from the doorway. I often
felt that stench, but if I had felt it only once I never
should forget it.

A morbid horror of this disease haunted me like a
nightmare, and every time I felt the stench of it I
imagined I was stricken with it. This horror of mine
was aggravated by the conduct of my mother, who
went into the pest-stricken houses, helped to lay out
the dead bodies, accompanied them to the graveyard,
and on one occasion even rode back in the hearse.
I shuddered to think she might convey the disease
into our house, but she told me that none caught it

except they were afraid of it ; and this assurance made me more afraid than ever ; and though I escaped, I was obsessed with the dread of it for years afterwards.

My mother plumed herself vastly on being able to read and write—a distinction that placed her far above the majority of our neighbours, and she was determined that I should share the same distinction. I remember her saying that it would be as hard for a bird to fly without wings as for a person to rise in the world without education. Toddling to school is one of my earliest recollections ; but even before then I had learned the alphabet, and never remember being in the position of one of our neighbours who boasted that he knew all the A.B.C.'s by sight if not by name.

The first school I went to was rather a funny one, and in these days of palatial schoolrooms, it seems hardly possible to imagine the sort of schools that existed in Ireland in my childhood's days. Barns and stable lofts were in common use for that purpose ; mine was neither the one nor the other, but something still more insanitary and uncomfortable. Situated only a few doors from our house, and kept by an old man dignified with the title of " Masther Canavan," the school was held in an apartment which served for both kitchen and living-room. It was there the food was cooked and eaten and the washing done, and not only that, but a loom which filled one side of the apartment was worked all day long by the master's daughter, a poor, consumptive girl called Phoebe. And what with the " clitterdy, clatterdy " of the loom, and the weaver's agonising fits of coughing, the pupils, or scholars as they called us, were cut off from the luxury of whispering. We numbered about a dozen, and sat around the turf fire, some on stools and some on a low form, while the master himself enjoyed the dignity of a chair. For the privilege of getting near the fire in the winter each pupil had to bring a few pieces of peat every morning, and the school fees were one penny per week, which was sometimes supplemented by an extra penny.

It was here I learned to spell and read, and I well remember commencing with A-B, Ab, B-O-T, Bot, " Abbot," and was mighty proud when I got as far as G-R-E-N, Gren, A-D-I-E-R, adier, " grenadier." I have also a very vivid remembrance of our dear old *Reading Made Easy*, or, as we called it, " Ready me Daisy," and groping my way through the sad story of Brown, Jones, Smith, and Robinson, the four naughty boys that went to bathe in the river instead of going to school.

In teaching handwriting, the kitchen table served for our desk, though it was seldom used as such ; and to read handwriting was considered the highest round in our ladder of learning. I remember how on one occasion the good master, with a touch of pardonable pride, boasted that one of his scholars had distinguished himself by reading a letter from America, or as he put it, a " Merrikay letter." He told us with much glee the case of another scholar, not, to be sure, one of his, who used to boast of his handwriting, and was asked by some friends to write a letter to America at their dictation. When he had finished it they asked him to read it. " But the sorra a word of it could he make out, so he folded it up with the remark : ' Sure it doesn't matter in the laist ; they'll be able to read it in Amerikay ; they're better scholars there than we are.' "

Writing in those days, and indeed for many a

year afterwards, was considered the *ne plus ultra* of learning. I remember even in the year 1870, one of my workmates telling me of an extraordinary example of learning that he knew ; it was that of a man who had been going to school up till the phenomenal age of eighteen. " He must have been a wonderful scholar when he left," said I. " Aye, man, so ye might well say ; why, he cud hae ta'en the pen between his two toes and wrote his name like copperplate."

My schooldays under Master Canavan were of short duration and sad ending. His daughter Phoebe grew worse and worse, and her cough often rose above the clatter of the loom. And when the loom would stop for a moment, a furtive glance might enable us to see that the poor creature would be wiping the blood from her mouth ; and at such times the poor old father would turn his back on " the scholars," take off his spectacles, rub them carefully with his handkerchief, and blow his nose as if he had suddenly caught a cold. Young as the scholars were they knew well what it all meant, and there was no disposition to laugh amongst them.

It soon came to an end ; one night Phoebe died after a flow of blood more profuse than usual, and her father closed the school, never again to open it. He survived her for a few weeks only, and during that time the neighbours ministered to his wants, even though they could very ill afford to do so.

Poor old Master, peace be to thy shade ! After the lapse of sixty odd years, thy form arises before me. With a scanty wisp of white hair and white side whiskers framing thy pinched and pallid features, and with thy bent figure tightly encased in a threadbare, but well-brushed, swallow-tailed black coat,

thou wert surely what thy neighbours called thee :
" The remains of ould daicency."

I was next sent to an " Infant School," conducted
under the auspices of the Protestant Establishment,
with the rector and curate as managers.   Although
my mother was one of the strictest of Catholics she
would not allow any sectarian prejudice to stand in
the way of my education, and very wisely considered
that learning was a fruit well worth the picking, no
matter what soil it grew upon.   I was too young to
go to the " National " school, which was some considerable distance away, while I had only to cross
the street to reach this school.   It was kept by a
Miss Madden, whose prim face, corkscrew ringlets,
and sever correctness of manner typified all the
conventionalities of the early Victorian period.   But
in spite of this formal appearance one could often
detect a twinkle of genial humour in her dark eyes,
and I rather fancy she took a kindly interest in myself.

The school fee of one penny per week she never
took from me, but said it had been paid already.

At this school I made good progress in reading,
and was soon able to read the Testament without a
mistake.   On one occasion the mistress offered a
prize of twopence to any child who would commit
to memory and repeat the parable of the " Seven
Wise and the Seven Foolish Virgins," and I became
the happy recipient of that prize.

Although the school was a Protestant institution,
and I was the only Catholic attending it, no attempt
was ever made to proselytise me, and I was never
asked to learn the Church Catechism, or to join in
prayer with the other children ; and this tolerance
predisposed me far more in favour of their creed
than any dogmas they could have ground into me.

I was really very sorry when this good lady left the school, but soon found I had no reason to be, for her successor, a Miss MacDonald, had all her excellence as a teacher, but none of her severe manner ; so it was no wonder that her amiability and good looks soon attracted the admiration of one of our promising young townsmen, and a happy marriage was the result. She still continued to teach, and I still continued her pupil until her first-born was able to walk, and she honoured me by putting the little chap to sit next to me.

I suppose I was then getting on to eight, and considered fit to walk to the National School, which was under the patronage of our parish priest, who suggested the change, and promised to be responsible for the fees of one penny per week. The school was kept by a master called Mickey Lappin, and all the pupils called him " Mickey," never " Master." He was considered an excellent teacher, for he never spared the rod and spoilt the child. He used to say : " The bird that can sing and won't sing I will make him sing," and " If I can't thrash the larnin' into a boy I can thrash the divil out of him ; " and he seldom failed to carry out these promises by means of a formidable hazel rod. It must not be imagined that the pupils always submitted with the meekness of angels. On the contrary, they harassed him with guerilla tactics, in which ink-bottles were the favourite weapons. Thus, if he inadvertently turned his back on the enemy a well-aimed blow from one of these missiles would remind him that perpetual vigilance is the price of despotic authority.

The school was a mixed one in every sense of the word, for not only was it composed of boys and girls, but of Catholics and Protestants. The effect of such an intermingling is even now a matter of controversy amongst educationalists. Its supporters, who are chiefly found in the New World, say that it has a refining influence on the boys and tends to develop their chivalrous instincts, and at the same time it corrects the diffidence of the girls and removes the consciousness of inequality. Be that as it may, I saw no trace of such influence amongst my fellow-schoolboys ; but amongst the girls diffidence was not only corrected, but almost entirely removed, for not content with equality they seemed to aim at mastery and were foremost in all the hoydenish fun that was carried on.

The intermingling of the sects was attended by the happiest results, inasmuch as it allowed the young people to understand one another, and contract friendships which no subsequent surroundings, or whisperings of bigotry, could ever wholly efface. It tended to bridge over the hideous gulf that has so long divided the people of Ulster into two hostile camps where the real interests of the common country are sacrificed to the delusions of a frenzied fanaticism.

It was the custom in the school for the boys to wear their hats and caps, the girls only going bareheaded ; and the master, with all his severity, didn't seem to mind this flagrant breach of discipline.

He had a favourite theory which I heard him propound more than once—it was to the effect that if Ireland were only surrounded with a wall of copper twelve feet high it would grow tobacco, and become the richest country in the world. He never explained why the wall should be of copper, and why it should be twelve feet high, but, to do him justice, he never blamed the Government for neglecting to build such a wall. He was a podgy man with a protuberant abdomen, a nose of the genus pug, very red and bulbous, dark hair and side whiskers, which were then fashionable, and may still be seen on the stage lawyer. It would be impossible not to consider him highly respectable, for he wore a black swallow-tailed coat, and never missed Mass on a Sunday or holiday, and he was eminently successful as a teacher, if, as many parents think, success depends on the use of the rod which they themselves never experienced as they probably deserved. He emigrated with his wife and family to Australia, and his pupils wished the Australians luck of their acquisition.

To him succeeded Stephen Porter, or Step-hen, as we used to call him. He was quite a different style of man from Mickey. He was not only wee in stature, but was also such a featherweight that we used to joke about dragging him to the fireplace to see whether the draught of the chimney would draw him up. For all his smallness he was an excellent disciplinarian, and, with less severity, he was able to win more respect than his predecessor. If two boys came to blows in the school, a matter of frequent occurrence, he sent them outside to fight it out to a finish, and when they tired of hammering each other, and came in, probably with two bloody noses, he would make them shake hands and promise to become friends, and friendships made in this way often became the most lasting.

With dark eyes, straight blue-black hair, beardless face, and lemon-coloured skin, he was more like a Malay than a European, while his mouth was never without a quid of tobacco. In spite of all his drawbacks, and even in spite of his frequent drinking bouts, Stephen was an excellent teacher as far as the three " R's " were concerned, with geography, grammar, and mensuration thrown in.

Like his predecessor, he had a pet theory that he hammered into us ; it was to the effect that birds were able to fly, not entirely because they had wings, but because their bones were filled with air instead of marrow ; and men would never be able to fly—no, not even if they had wings—until the marrow was extracted from their bones and air substituted.

Of all the pupils who floundered about in grammar, I doubt if there was a single one who looked upon it otherwise than a meaningless jargon ; and as for parsing—well, that was a bewildering maze that led nowhere. I remember one boy had the hardihood to ask the master what was the use of it all ? And the master, after dislodging a quid from his mouth, as he usually did before answering a question, replied : "You will know the use of it when you grow up."

I got on very well with him, and was soon in the fourth class, which was the highest in the school. I was also considered one of the best readers in the school and best able to give the meaning of the words I read, so I was generally trotted out to show off when the priest or inspector paid us a visit.

For all my progress I was lazy and negligent as far as lessons were concerned, but I was obsessed with a positive mania for reading all the books I could lay hands on, hence my proficiency in the knowledge of words. This passion for reading began I know not how ; far earlier in my life than I can remember, and in face of difficulties which seemed insurmountable, grew stronger as I grew older ; and I doubt if any human being ever possessed it in a greater degree or made more desperate efforts to indulge in it. It has been the charm of my existence —the sunshine that converted the gloomiest of prospects into a paradise where my imagination luxuriated amongst the richest fruits and fairest flowers of the human intellect, while the squalid realities that surrounded me were lost in the divinest of all companionships.

After my sixty-eight years experience of life, I vow that if I had the option of being born again, and the Great Giver of Life offered me a choice of gifts on my coming into the world, I would choose neither wealth nor power, nor any other prize that attracts the majority of mankind.—No ; my choice would be the love of books.

I believe the first book I ever read while still at the Infant School was the *History of Sandford and Merton*, and this was followed by the *History of Susan Gray*—the story of a virtuous housemaid and a profligate captain, told in the lachrymose style, well buttered with scriptural quotations, so dear to the hearts of our pious grandmothers.

At the National School this passion of mine was devouring me, whilst the opportunities of gratifying it were in the inverse ratio. I used to procure tops, marbles, kites, and whatever playthings were popular amongst my schoolmates, and with these treasures I would tempt them to steal any old books they might find at home and lend them to me. When I got any book that had to be returned within a limited time, I would " mitch " from school and hide in a loft over our kitchen, and then spend the livelong day lost to everything in the delight of enjoying my feast. When I happened to get a good haul in poetry, such as the *Robin Hood Ballads* or *The Lay of the Last Minstrel*, I would usually commit it to memory. These were the first two poetry books that fell into my hands, and many passages from them still live in my memory.   c

My next haul in verse consisted of Dryden's *Virgil* and Pope's *Homer*, and in prose, Goldsmith's *Citizen of the World*, which has never lost the high place it then won in my esteem, or perhaps I should say affection.

The master soon observed my passion, and looked upon it with a sympathetic eye. Being the happy owner of a few old books, he kindly put them at my disposal, and I reciprocated with my treasures.

Like his predecessor, Mickey Lappin, he gave up the school, and with his wife and family emigrated to Australia. I had left the school some time before he left the country, and had lent him one of my greatest treasures—an odd volume of the *Spectator*, in return for some odd numbers of the *London Journal*, containing *Ivanhoe*, illustrated by Sir John Gilbert. But these I had unfortunately lent to another friend, by whom they were lost ; I was then confronted with the problem of how I should recover my *Spectator* from Master Stephen without returning his *London Journals*, for, of course, I could not go and ask him to return my loan without returning his at the same time. So I resorted to stratagem. One fine summer evening a few days before he left, I strolled up, casually as it were, past his house, which was some distance from the town, and seeing his son Dan at the door, I approached him, and pointing to a cluster of cottages a little way off, I asked him in which of them Ned Toner the thatcher lived, as my mother wanted him to do some work. Dan, of course, gladly obliged me by pointing out the house, and after loitering around it for a few minutes, I returned, and again accosted Dan, and, struck as it were with a sudden thought, said that as I chanced to be passing, I might as well take back my book, and thus save them the trouble of sending it to me ; as regarded the *London Journals* it had never occurred to me that I should see him or I should certainly have brought them back. I would, however, be sure to do so before the family left. I very much fear that this promise is still against me in the Recording Angel's big book. A few nights after I heard a tremendous knocking at our door, but fortunately the kitchen was in darkness, and if the knocking had continued from that day till this, my guilty conscience would have prevented me from answering.

During my stay at this school, when I had exhausted all the supply of old books which my schoolmates were able to pilfer for me, I went as a new pupil to the Church school, and ingratiated myself into the favour of the boys there, and set them to hunt, as my new set of jackals. This move did not come up to my expectations, for the only books they could procure for me were of a religious sort which I merely sniffed at and dishonoured by returning. At the end of a fortnight I went back to my old school, where I was admitted without any questions. In those happy-go-lucky days there were no school attendance officers.

During all my school days I was never once guilty of wearing shoes and stockings, but I can hardly boast of this as a merit, for it was a matter of necessity, not choice. After all, this custom is far more healthy than that which prevails in the slums of English cities, where one may see poor children go to school in old boots of all shapes and sizes with soles and uppers ready to part company and freely admitting water and mud in which the benumbed feet are soaked all day long. As for the rest of my schoolday

attire, it consisted of " hand-me-downs " picked up
by second-hand clothes dealers in the slums of
Glasgow ; I remember wearing for a very long time
an old uniform jacket given me by a revenue policeman, and at another time a pair of corduroy knee-
breeches, the cast-offs of an overgrown butcher, and
big enough to cover my whole body, let alone my
poor, wee legs. Although I have worn heaps of
outlandish toggery, these are the only two articles I
have ever felt ashamed of, although the row of brass
buttons on the front of the jacket made me the envy
of all my schoolmates.

When I left school I had made such a reputation
for scholarship that I was in universal request
amongst the neighbours to write their letters, not
only to England or Scotland, but even to America.
This was a commission that I appreciated very much,
for it generally procured me a cup of tea and a slice
of white bread, for so baker's bread was called
amongst us.

These letters invariably began with the pious
formula : " Dear So-and-so, I take up my pen to
write you these few lines hoping they will find you
in good health as they leave us at the present, thanks
be to God for His kind mercies to us all ! " I wrote
them word for word, and always had to read them
at the end to show that I had done my work faithfully.
Another work that my scholarship entailed upon me
was reading at wakes. I was wont to be accommodated
with a chair as close as possible to the head of the
corpse, and given a prayer-book from which I would
read the Seven Penitential Psalms with an affected
solemnity that touched the hearts of all the old
women around me ; and if these were more pious
than usual, as indeed they usually were, I had to

continue my performance through " Prayers for the Dead," by way of an encore.

Like all things connected with Ireland and described by those who know nothing about them, descriptions of wakes are for the most part hideous caricatures. I have seen as many of them as most people, but I have never seen the riotous fun that has been described as going on within them. I have, to be sure, seen a subdued sort of fun and heard many jokes and much badinage, called " sconcing," amongst the young folk around the kitchen fire or in some room apart from the one where the corpse was laid out ; but in presence of the dead, reverent restraint was the rule.

The gruesomest story I ever heard about a wake reached me from the town of Coleraine, so douce and enlightened in the eyes of its inhabitants, one of whom told me the story and vouched for its truth.

In a lonely cabin on the outskirts of the town lived two women—mother and daughter—of such evil repute that none but the very worst characters ever crossed their threshold. And so it came to pass that when the mother died, not a soul came to the wake except a plasterer and a chimney sweep—the two champion blackguards of the town. While they were there the daughter, worn out with watching, went to sleep on the loft over the kitchen and left the two worthies by themselves at a blazing turf fire with the corpse in the same apartment. Being thus left to their own devices for beguiling the time, they decided to play cards, but before commencing found they had no money to play for ; when the sweep made the horrible and blasphemous suggestion that his companion, whose clothes were spotted white with plaster, should personate God Almighty, while, as his own garments were of the opposite colour, he would personate the devil, and they would play for " the sowl " of the dead woman. Captivated with this brilliant idea, they set to, and after a rubber of " twenty-five," the popular Irish game, the sweep became the winner. He then swore a dreadful oath that he would not carry off the prize until he would see how she could stand the fire, and with these words, he dragged the dead woman out of the bed and stuck both her feet into the blazing turf fire.

The pungent smell of the burning flesh and the hissing and crackling sound that accompanied it soon filled the cabin and awoke the daughter from her slumber overhead, who, coming down the ladder, took in the situation in a horrified look. Having snatched up and replaced the dead body, she plumped down on her knees—" her bare knees," said my informant—and prayed to Heaven that the sweep might himself be roasted alive before the end of the year.

Sure enough, this actually took place, for soon afterwards, while tryng to save a burning cabin, he fell through the thatched roof and was burned to a cinder.

CHAPTER II

When I left school I was about eleven years old, and though intellectually more precocious, physically I was more puny than most boys of the same age. I had never played with other children nor taken the slightest interest in open-air games, and my only recreation was swimming, of which I was passionately fond. I have never witnessed a cricket match nor a game of football, and have never touched a billiard cue, and I am inclined to think there are few men in a civilised community could say as much in their sixty-eighth *anno Domini*. I do not, however, say it by way of boast, but rather as a matter of regret. It was a drawback that made me feel prematurely old, and conduced to priggishnesss and pedantry rather than expansion.

As soon as I left school I had to commence work, for my mother kept continually impressing me with the unanswerable argument that I was bound to work for my living all through life and the sooner I started the better. By " work " was meant manual labour, for mental labour was considered no work at all. Even manual labour was considered hardly more than a pleasant and profitable pastime when the labourer was his own master and pocketed all the profits ; but to work for " the stranger " was labour in earnest. Such, however, was my work, and it consisted of weeding crops of flax, oats, and potatoes, gleaning in the harvest fields, and gathering potatoes as they were dug up in the autumn. At this work I would be bent for ten and a half hours daily, and the employer usually stood over his gang allowing one no time to straighten the back.

How I used to thank Heaven when the rain came down and stopped the work, even though it stopped the pay as well, which in my case was sixpence a day ; for being only a small boy it could not of course be expected that I should get as much as a grown-up woman, whose pay was eightpence.

During all this time my craze for reading never abated, but rather seemed to become intensified the more difficulties it encountered. Working as I then did, there was little time to indulge in it, but even if the time were allowed the means were wanting. Books at that time were dear, for no enterprising publishers had arisen like ministering angels to unseal the fountains of Literature, and allow impecunious creatures like myself to indulge in delightful draughts at a cheap rate. In fact, the cheapest books that could be obtained were two-shilling novels by tenth-rate authors, presented in yellow covers flimsy, and flamboyant. These, however, were far beyond my finances, which seldom exceeded twopence, and on rare occasions, sixpence ; but when my small stock of books had been well perused I would hawk them around on market days, and sell them for any price I could get ; and in this way I sometimes raised the wind for the purchase of a few more.

When I had " begged, borrowed, or stolen " all the books of my neighbours, mainly through the agency of their boys whom I managed to wheedle, I became the client of one Joe Kelly, a strolling hawker in hardware trumperies, supplemented with old books, which he either sold at ridiculously high prices, or let out at twopence or threepence per

volume weekly. As often as I could afford the twopence I borrowed from him, and in this way became
acquainted with most of the novels that were popular
in those days, the authors being Fenimore Cooper,
Bulwer Lytton, Mayne Reid, Harrison Ainsworth,
Jane Porter, and so forth.

In my old age, I have often tried to renew the
delights of my boyhood by re-reading some of these
books. I regret to say I have in most cases found
it impossible to do so, and have been obliged to
throw aside the volume in utter weariness. The
only favourites of my youth which I am still able to
read with unabated delight are the novels of William
Carleton. They are photographs of Irish life in the
first half of the nineteenth century, which for realism,
humour, and pathos have never been equalled ; and
with them I would couple the works of Charles
Lever, especially his *Con Cregan*. Another book
which is still able to renew the delights of boyhood
is *The Adventures of Haji Baba of Ispahan*—a never-
failing tickler of my jaded palate. I was so fascinated
with this book that I kept it long over the allotted
week, and in fact would have kept it perpetually had
not Joe called at our house on a Saturday night and
insisted on my delivering it up ; which I felt like
the delivering up of my heart's blood. This man
had a very bad reputation amongst all well-meaning
parents as being a " deludherer " of their boys with
his " yeller-backed " seductions, and on this occasion
my mother, who met him for the first time, but had
often heard of him, gave him such a tongue-thrashing
that he hurried off with the fear of God in his heart
and never again lent her son a book.

After him, my next jackal was an eccentric character
called " Oiney Neill," or, as he called himself,

" Eugene O'Neill of the Bloody Hand and Dagger,"
alluding to the crest of the princes from whom he
claimed descent. He was a hawker of old books
only, and with these stuffed in a van which he lived
in, he used to travel around the country and attend
the various fairs and markets. His stock consistsd
of odd volumes, mostly eighteenth-century products,
dealing with all sorts of subjects, but above all
theological. It was a treat to watch Oiney sell his
wares by Dutch auction He would start a book,
say at five shillings, and run it down to twopence ;
and if he flung it down unsold in well-feigned desperation no offer would tempt him to pick it up and
part with it. He would say : " It has gone from
Purgatory into Heaven and there it must remain."
He would sell an old Bible or Prayer Book as " a
gun for shootin' the divil " ; an old almanack would
be " the lives of all the authentic characters—poets,
warriors, philosophers, and divines." Any old volume
in a foreign language would be the works of " Harry
Stottle showin' how to turn pot metal into goold,"
or, maybe, it would be " The Art of Raising the
Devil and making him do anything you want."

He had a truculent independence of manner that
was more amusing to witness than experience. He
would allow nobody, gentle or simple, to open his
books, or even touch them, and anyone trying to do
so would be immediately brought to his bearing with
the loud, imperative : " Drop that book, scabby head,
and go and scratch your granny." Every time he
came to our market I made a point of seeing him,
and would hang around his van on the look-out for
a bargain if I happened to be the happy possessor of
twopence—more than this I was never able to invest
with him at any one time. I would, indeed, have

given worlds to have made his acquaintance, and have the privilege—the inestimable privilege—of prowling amongst his treasures. He seemed as unapproachable as a wild bear, and I studied him all round, just as a general might study a strong fortress that he meant to capture.

As good luck would have it, I discovered that, like Achilles, he had a vulnerable spot—not indeed in his heel, but in his nose—in a word, he took snuff. I therefore armed myself with a pennyworth of this ammunition, and sauntering around his wares watched my opportunity for attracting his notice in an idle moment. When this occurred, I helped myself to a pinch, and approaching the great man said very deferentially : "Mister O'Neill, will you take a sneeshin'." Now, this speech, short as it seems, was carefully premeditated ; for he was intensely Irish, and if I had not put the O' to his name he would have considered himself shorn of his ancestral dignity ; and if I had said "pinch" instead of "sneeshin'" he would have looked upon me as a renegade who had discarded his native language. As it was, he accepted my "sneeshin'" and thanked me very graciously, but when I offered him all that remained he declined, saying he had plenty. I had tact enough not to attempt looking at his books just then, but went away congratulating myself on the progress made. I had good reason to do so, for on the following day, Sunday, he sent a message to me by one of my friends inviting me to look through his books. It is needless to say I was delighted, but the result was disappointing, for I never handled such heaps of rubbish. However, I succeeded in grubbing out an odd volume of the *Spectator*, one of Pope, and one of Dryden. These he let me have at my own price, namely, twopence each, and not only that, I might pay him at my convenience. That debt was not paid, for when he went away I never saw him again ; but if a grateful remembrance could have paid him he has been paid a hundred times over.

In those days I left no stone unturned to obtain the wherewithal for the gratification of my passion ; but the stones, alas ! were nearly always turned in vain. As our markets were held on Saturday, and big markets they then were, I used to get up at daybreak on the Sundays during the summer months and carefully search the market place for any coins that might have been dropped on the previous night ; but Providence on all these occasions never put any luck in my way. And in the evenings when I used to await the arrival of the train from Belfast, a similar disappointment awaited me, for I never earned a penny by getting a parcel to carry, though I never missed an opportunity of offering my services.

After many casual jobs of longer or shorter duration, sometimes as a field labourer, sometimes as an errand boy or newsboy, I at last got permanent employment from our ground landlord, or lord of the manor, as he would be called in England. My wages were to be three shillings a week, and this week was to include Sunday. He had been after building a " big house " surrounded with many acres of land levelled from the fields of his former tenants. On this land he had planted a vast number of young trees both singly and in clumps, and the rest of the land was grazing ground for at least a dozen of his cows.

It was my duty to watch these cows and see that they did not damage the young trees or break into the adjoining crops. Every morning I had to be on

the scene at six a.m., cleanse and currycomb their
hides, and at six p.m. I had to drive them in for the
night, arrange their beds, and supply them with
fodder. Watching these cattle gave me a lot of
trouble, for I could never keep them quite together,
and while I had one group under my eye others
would keep straying out of sight, and not a few
would attack the young trees with their horns,
seeming to say *Faugh an Ballagh*, or " Clear the
way," and so my legs were seldom at rest. But
when they did get a moment's rest I always whipped
out a book, with which my pocket was never un-
provided, and I soon became lost to all the mean
realities of my position.

But if I became lost to these realities my employer
was very much alive to them, and kept watching me
with an eye that was far from indulgent. After
being two and a half years in his service, during
which time I had never had a single day off, neither
Sunday nor holiday, nor even Christmas Day, he
put me to work in the yard, where I had to attend
the pigs and poultry, while the man who did that
work was sent to labour in the fields. The very
first day I was thus left alone I took the earliest
opportunity of squatting comfortably on a truss of
hay in the cowshed, and pulling out my book was
soon transported into the Elysian fields of Fancy,
which on this occasion were comprised in a dog-
eared copy of *Charles O'Malley*. During all the time
I was rapt in this enjoyment I little thought that the
eye of my employer was fixed upon me, as it really
was. He outmanœuvred me by a masterly piece of
strategy, and made a proud boast of it afterwards
amongst his men, that he had caught me very neatly
in the trap by concealing himself all day long in the

stable opposite, where the window commanded a view of my lair without allowing him to be seen. At the end of the week my mother got notice that another week would terminate the engagement of her good-for-nothing son.

All our neighbours considered my dismissal a terrible misfortune for which I alone was to blame. If I had been only a " smart " boy and attended to my work it was " sure and sartin " that I should have found favour in the big man's eyes and been promoted from the yard to the kitchen, and maybe in the long run have been raised to the high and mighty position of his butler. Now, such a promotion was of all things in the world that which I most loathed and detested, for like the majority of the Irish peasants, I considered the position of a flunkey most mean and unmanly. There was, to be sure, nothing mean or unmanly in waiting on the cows and pigs of " his honour " ; but to wait on himself and wear his livery—well, there ! To me it seemed specially degrading, for my mother had repeatedly drilled it into me that I must consider myself as good as anybody else and never lower my colours to " the face of clay."

This spur to the good opinion I had formed of myself was absolutely unnecessary ; for did I not live in a world infinitely exalted over that of my employer ? I not only moved amongst the lords and ladies of fiction, but shared the companionship of the greatest and best characters that radiate in history and brighten the memory of mankind. In short, to have purchased me at my own estimate would have made a millionaire bankrupt, especially if he had sold me at the estimate of my employer.

" Big Jimmy," as my employer was called by his

men, would have been reckoned an extraordinary character anywhere outside of Ulster ; there he was quite a common type. He had made a lot of money as a linen bleacher on a large scale and took advantage of the Encumbered Estates Act to buy up the greater part of our town and all the available land around it, on which he employed a large number of labourers. He was the very *beau idéal* of a slave-driver. Every blessed morning, summer and winter, he would be up and about at six a.m. to see that his hands had duly arrived, and to escort them to the scene of the day's labour. During all the rest of the day he would stand over them without intermission, save the half-hour for breakfast and the whole hour for dinner from one till two p.m. Every second Friday he would break this rule and take his seat on the magisterial bench, where, I am glad to say, he was neither bigoted nor unjust. Indeed, he never discriminated in the employment of labourers, but engaged Catholics quite as readily as Protestants— an impartiality which was by no means common amongst his brother magnates.

During the two and a half years I worked for him I never had a single day's rest, and had to be in the yard every morning at six a.m. Throughout the winter months this was long before daylight, and as we had neither clock nor watch I would usually get up after the first sleep, between three and four a.m., and sit reading until I heard the horn to awaken the mill workers blown through the street at five a.m., which would give me an idea of the time to set off for my work. This habit of early rising stuck on me many, many years, and it was during such hours that I did the greater part of my reading. All through the years of work I felt too tired at the end of the day to sit up late, so I always made up for early retiring by early rising. It was, indeed, remarked by our townspeople that no one amongst them could rise early enough to find young Mullin's window without a light in it ; the said light being emitted from a tin lamp filled with paraffin oil, and shaped like a teapot with the wick coming up through the spout, on the same principle as terracotta lamps of the most remote antiquity.

About this time I was smitten with a passionate love of poetry, mainly imbibed from the poems of Robert Burns—an idol whom I took to my heart and never dethroned—even after reading his letters. In this respect he seemed to me the antithesis of Cowper, whose poetry, as wholesome and as heavy as suet pudding, I can always tolerate for the sake of his delightful letters.

From idolising to imitating was an easy transition, especially under the stimulus of puerile vanity, and the result was sundry atrocious imitations of my idol which might have disheartened a less persevering wooer of the muse than myself. Looking at it from my present standpoint, I doubt whether I would ever have gone so far in this wooing if I could have foreseen what lay before me. I might probably have calculated that it would pay me much better to take up the study of Mathematics, in which I was destined to prove such a duffer.

I suppose, however, I followed the course Nature intended, and am sure I would have persevered in it had I remained a workman ; but I feel a wee bit sorry to say that when I became a university scholar, the strictness of the course I was compelled to pursue narrowed my views, and so I dismounted, at least for the time being, from the hobby that gave me more pleasure than profit. And yet, if Nature had meant me to be a poet I should have stuck to my hobby and thrown all other tasks to the dogs.

I had timidly sent to a Dublin paper, called *The Irishman*, some patriotic verses in imitation of " Scots Wha Hae," and, impossible as it seemed, felt vainer than ever when they duly appeared in all the glory of print.

Always when I got a new poet into my hands I used to set about imitating him, which fact in itself, if I had been less vain, might have convinced me I was not a born poet, for I drew no inspiration from Nature, and neither felt nor affected the passion of Love. The only books of verse I could obtain were odd volumes of the eighteenth century—products of a period when everybody wrote verse and nobody, comparatively speaking, wrote poetry. These were as easy of imitation as grinding music out of a hurdy-gurdy, and so I covered heaps of paper with monotonous heroic couplets, which, *mirabile dictu*, I had sense enough to burn. But if I admired the eighteenth century heroics I admired still more the satires of the same period and imitated them with greater pleasure, so that from the general holocaust I was tempted to save a few.

But my effusion in *The Irishman* and some others that, like Sir Benjamin Backbite's, " circulated in manuscript," won for me the title of " Poet," a title which was not always complimentary. For with the good people I lived amongst, so far from signifying any intellectual pre-eminence, it signified an instability of character and a deficiency of those solid qualities that ensure prosperity and command respect. Conscious that I did not deserve the title either in a good or bad sense, I always resented it, and never allowed

D

anyone to tickle my vanity by using it in my presence without letting him feel he had made a mistake. Instead of braying in the lion's skin to the amusement of the onlooker, the ass invariably asserted his dignity and disconcerted the onlooker with an unpleasant kick.

In Ireland, above all countries, when one gets a nickname it is sure to stick, and stick all the longer the more it is resented. It was so in my case until I became sensible enough to take it in good part as a contribution to my amusement. But what disgusted me so much was to find that the title bestowed on me was also bestowed on two of my neighbours by whom it was flaunted as a mighty big honour. One of these was our neighbour, Tammy Dooris, whose tastes outsoared his vocation, which was that of a labourer, and the other was " Pluck " Murray, a rag and bone collector. Why he was called " Pluck " I never knew, but I know that he resented it, and always insisted on being called " Lord Murray," as he claimed to be a scion of Scottish nobility. Although I, who had appeared in print, spurned comparison with these competitors for the local laureateship, such comparisons were often made, somewhat on the following lines : " Well, it's just like this ; Tammy cud make a scarecrow shake the duds off his back laughing, an' Pluck cud make ye feel as miserable as a monkey mournin' for his mother-in-law ; but, begobs, wee Jemmy cud knock the wind out o' ye wi' the dictionary." Now, although this was meant as a compliment to myself, I felt it cut two ways.

Pluck, like his rival, Tammy, was an improvisator ; and both made the publichouse, especially on Saturday night, the stage for the display of their genius ; and it was well worth anyone's while who had a sense of humour to wet their whistles with a few drinks and hear them reel out their rhymes like one o'clock. I rather think that Pluck's pathos caused more merriment than Tammy's humour, except in one case that fairly took the cake. This was Tammy's masterpiece—a ballad, or should I say an epic, composed on a wonderful sow belonging to a farmer known as " Red Brogues," from the fact that his brogues were always coated with red clay. This sow was a terror to the neighbourhood. She could insinuate herself through the smallest opening in the thickest hedge, level a dry stone fence with her shoulder, or upset a wooden paling with her snout. No crop, either above ground or below, was safe from her depredations, for where she failed to root up and devour, she always succeeded in trampling down. She got " Red Brogues " involved in so many quarrels with his neighbours that at last he was obliged to put her under a coercion act. This materialised in a collar placed around her neck, shaped as a triangle, out of sticks that projected a long way out at each angle so as to effectually prevent her from pushing through gaps except of the very widest dimensions. Her career of conquest was thus cut short, and as she hobbled around under this portable Caudine Fork, she tickled Tammy's fancy so hugely that he made her the subject of his great masterpiece, and turned her degradation into her glory.

I once heard Tammy's gifted rival, Lord Murray, do a piece of improvisation which, in the beautiful language of some of the audience, was " enough to charm the heart of a wheelbarrow." It happened that some of the " prime boys " of our town found

his lordship in a condition specially favourable to
the divine afflatus. Taking advantage of the occasion,
they put him into a donkey cart, wheeled him all
round the town to the accompaniment of a handbell,
which drew an immense crowd. At every house
where an unpopular individual resided, the procession
would halt, and the poet at the top of his voice
declaim a doggerel rhyme castigating some physical
defect, moral delinquency, or social scandal connected
with the unfortunate inmate.

I remember taking part in the procession and
enjoying immensely the sallies of " his lordship,"
and even felt moved to emulate him, *sub rosa*. I
therefore drew up a black list of my fellow
townsmen and stigmatised each of them in a couplet
intended to make them dance without the aid of
music, while I chuckled inwardly at the performance.
Now, so far from having any grievance or ill will
against any of these good people I would have done
them a good turn if I could, and I am quite sure
they would have done the same to me. I merely
set them up as targets to shoot my rhymes against
for the sake of amusement, just as a mischievous boy
might amuse himself by flinging mud at them in the
dark.

From the cemetery of my memory where many
more valuable things have been long buried in
oblivion, I venture to disinter a few specimens of
" My Portrait Gallery " :

THE LOOSE-LIPPED PUBLICAN

A baby pig would think itself in luck
If put at Gabby's open mouth to suck.

THE KNOCK-KNEED BARBER
Jock's knees don't act as brother should to brother,
But try to knock the brains out of each other.

THE LONG-WINDED ORATOR
Dick Swab would be the wisest of mankind,
If Wisdom were identical with Wind.

ON THE AUTHOR
Our author is a rather pert young prig,
His wit is small as his conceit is big,
He has the Devil's own amount of cheek,
But all he earns is three bob a week !

The last portrait was as true to life as any of the others, of which there were about a dozen, and in thus castigating myself I compounded for the thrashing which my conscience told me I had richly deserved. But, after all, my conscience was too sensitive, for I exaggerated the importance of my lampoons ; few ever saw them and nobody ever minded them.

Indeed, I have never formed a bad opinion of any human being without regretting, or at least modifying it, afterwards ; and the pleasant scurrilities of my youth have been the bitterest memories of my old age.

Such were some of my earliest efforts at wooing the Muse, for whom my passion was like that of a man for a beautiful woman who reciprocates far less warmly than he wishes ; but nevertheless he persists in pressing his suit, and for the chance of an occasional smile puts up with many a frown. In my case, though the frowns far exceeded the smiles, the passion remained quiescent, it might be for a few years, under the pressure of hard work, but always broke out when that pressure was removed and manifested itself in effusions on divers subjects and of diverse lengths. Many of them appeared anonymously in local papers, and many of them were born to blush unseen. Although this hobby afforded me much recreation, it never led me to indulge in any dreams of winning poetic distinction. I had just as much of the poet in my nature as spoiled me from being a successful plodder, and just as much of the plodder as prevented me from being a poet.

But, to revert to my working life, when " Big Jemmy " invested me with his order of the sack, I was more delighted than was ever royal favourite with the Order of the Garter, for I fondly imagined I could never fall into the hands of a worse master nor encounter a prospect more degrading than his servitude. In this I was vastly deceived.

My next employment was with the second husband of my father's widowed sister, living in the good old town of Dungannon, nine miles from my own town. Originally a butcher, he rose to the position of cattle dealer, exporting to the English markets the brutes that I considered less brutal than himself; and if this opinion has long since given place to a more charitable one it took many years to effect the change. If Big Jemmy, my late employer, acted as a slave driver, it was only to get value for the wage he was paying me ; but here was another Big Jemmy, my uncle, too, who not only gave me no wage, but acted as my tormentor, apparently from sheer love of making me wretched and humbling me to the gutter. If I were not in the field watching his cattle, he would put me to the dirtiest work imaginable, such as boiling down putrid and stinking flesh to feed his

pigs, and cleaning his yard, which was virtually an
open cesspool. I dare not sit down in his presence,
and my looking at a book would almost drive him
into a fit of homicidal mania. But, indeed, there
were no books in his house except old almanacs,
and I used to find consolation in these by committing
to memory the dates of the births and deaths of
great men and the leading events of history. He
would not even let me sleep, but would keep me up
till the latest hour, and then rouse me up at the first
glimpse of dawn, getting up for the moment to do
so. Neither would he allow me to have my meals
until he had finished eating, and then I might sit
down to his leavings.

Although this custom of feeding servants was then
rather common amongst middle-class people in
Ireland, and implied no insult, to me, who did not
consider myself a servant, it seemed not only in-
sulting, but degrading and disgusting, and made my
blood boil with indignation. I am glad to say I
never once submitted to it, but when my uncle was
at home I would purchase a pennyworth of bread at
the baker's and make a meal of that. When he was
absent at the fairs I had meals with my aunt, who
kindly informed me that I was a " wee bit saft in
the head," and that I ought to pray fervently to the
Almighty to cure me of pride, which was a mortal
sin, and, unabsolved, would damn me for ever. My
uncle, on the other hand, told her behind my back
that he did not want a gentleman in his house. She
agreed with him, and I agreed with them both, and
scuttled back to my mother as fast as my feet would
carry me, after spending a month in a way that would
make the same period in a convict prison seem
blissful.

When I got home my mother treated me to a wigging, not, indeed, for leaving, but for leaving without dashing in my uncle's face " the dirty lavings " I was offered, just as she would have done, and as I should have done if I had had any spirit in me.

Well, if I had done so I should have got the worst of the bargain, for he was a big, powerful man, and his ferocity was still greater than his bodily strength. I cannot resist the temptation of telling an incident which illustrates this, and at the same time throws a lurid light on the state of party feeling that prevailed in Ulster at that time ; and which unhappily still prevails, though kept, perhaps, under better control.

In those days there existed, and perhaps still exists, if under another name, in the neighbourhood of Dungannon a body of Orangemen, popularly called the " Killymoon Wreckers," from a playful habit they had of going around the country at night and wrecking the houses of obnoxious Papists. Now, these gentlemen decided to march through Dungannon, and in full war paint, with their fifes and drums, frighten the sowls out of the Teagues, as the Irish Catholics were nicknamed when England went mad singing " Lilli Burlero." Nay, they would not only walk through the principal streets, but they swore by the memory of the Boyne that they would walk even through Shamble Lane, the headquarters of the butchers ; and these were not only Teagues, but Teagues of the most fanatical and ferocious type, and amongst them none was more so than my precious uncle.

When the stalwarts of Shamble Lane heard that their sanctum was about to be profaned by a procession of the Yellowbellies they pledged themselves by " the ten crosses of Christ " that such a profanation should never occur except over their dead bodies. Accordingly, when the day of action arrived they drew a chalked line across the entrance of their land, and behind the line they stood, drawn up in battle array, armed with knives, hatchets, and cleavers, all newly sharpened for the work before them. When the Wreckers came up, they were rather taken aback at this display, and halted, but one of them, bolder than the rest, made a spring at the point where my uncle had taken his stand with a hatchet on his shoulder. No sooner had he done so than my uncle raised his hatchet, and with a blow that would have felled an ox, clove his skull, bespattering the pavement with a mixture of brain matter and blood. This example impressed the others with the fact that discretion is the better part of valour, and so they departed, leaving the butchers to crow on their own dunghill.

My uncle, of course, was arrested, tried for manslaughter, and got two years hard labour. It was, however, to his credit that he not only never boasted of the affair, but never allowed it to be mentioned in his presence.

CHAPTER III

When I returned home from the month's enjoyment of my uncle's hospitality, I had to set about seeking new employment, and, without letting my mother know, I went to the local weaving factory and got a start at winding bobbins for the weavers, being too small to start on a loom. At this work I remained only one week, when my mother insisted on my leaving it without waiting to give notice or receive pay. She reasoned with me that if I stayed in the factory I should never be able to earn big wages, even if my health kept good, which was by no means certain ; and that even if the wages should become big, the monotony of the work would ultimately make me no better than a portion of the machine I worked with ; so that I should ultimately lose all prospect of striking out for myself in any independent path of life. Once a factory hand always a factory hand—a mere mechanism for putting money in the master's pocket, with hope and ambition strangled in the deadly routine that absorbs the attention and leaves no outlook beyond the daily task. These, of course, were not her exact words, but this was the purport of the words she used, which coincided exactly with my own line of reasoning.

She insisted, moreover, that I must learn a trade, for a trade, she declared, would make me independent no matter what part of the world I should go to. With a trade I could snap my fingers at Fortune and never degenerate into a loafer or become a sponger ; it would prevent me from falling in the world, but never prevent me from rising, for, of course, I could lay it aside if the chance of rising offered itself.

The next point was to decide what trade I should learn ; but here the choice was exceedingly restricted. There were no soft trades in our town, but even if there had been I had neither the influence nor the means to get pushed into one of them. I had nothing to choose beyond becoming a shoemaker, a tailor, a blacksmith, or a carpenter. The first two I disliked owing to the conditions under which they were carried on—conditions that seemed to me rather cramping and confining both to body and mind and likely to impede my healthy development. For the third I was too puny, and so my choice fell on carpentry.

My mother approved of this choice, remarking that our Saviour in working at it had made it the divinest of all handicrafts.

Now, there were two branches of carpentry in our town, one being house carpentry or joinery, and the other cart carpentry, which was confined to the making of carts, ploughs, and other farming implements, with the making of coffins occasionally thrown in. The joiners were all fairly well paid and their work was comparatively light and clean, while the cart makers, on the other hand, were poorly paid— few of them being able to earn more than ten shillings a week, and their work rough and heavy. They were, in fact, the Plebeian workmen, the others the Patrician who looked down upon them from inaccessible heights.

As I had no influence to get apprenticed to the joinery work I had to tackle the cartmaking, where no influence was required, as the work was not considered worth it. To this, then, I was apprenticed for a term of five years, during which I was to receive half-a-crown a week, without either food or clothing. At the end of five years if I became a good workman I had a fair prospect of earning ten shillings a week, but this would be the maximum. The terms of my apprenticeship were merely verbal. No indentures were drawn up and no bond asked for, the reason being that I was considered too unpromising to be worth such an arrangement, for my master, no doubt, assumed that my running away would be no loss to him.

At this trade I remained nine years under circumstances as adverse and with prospect as gloomy as Fate could inflict on any man outside a prison. But though these years left me with a bent back and grey hairs at the age of twenty-two, they left me with no regrets for wasted time or lost opportunities, and I doubt whether I should shirk them if I had the chance of doing so in a new life. They sharpened whatever small wits I possessed, hardened my powers of endurance, and filled me with confidence in wrestling with adversity. So far from diminishing my passion for books they strengthened it, even as the passion of a lover is strengthened by the difficulties he encounters in meeting his mistress.

My new master was another specimen of the Ulster slave driver, but not to his workmen more than to himself, for he always set them an example of what he expected them to do—an example that I always admired and never followed. His work seemed the very breath of his nostrils. When we entered the workshop at six a.m. we always found him at work before us, and when we left at six, or rather seven p.m., we always left him at work after us. If, too, there was one job harder than another, in the way of sawing, hacking, or hammering, he would invariably take that job in hand. We were supposed to begin work at six a.m. and end at six p.m. with a half-hour's rest for breakfast and a whole hour for dinner ; but these working hours were only nominal, for the journeymen, headed by his brother never left off before 6.30 p.m. ; and I myself, the unfortunate apprentice, seldom got off before seven or eight p.m. or until such time as he chose to let me. He would generally give me a fresh piece of work before closing time and say : " Now then, let us hurry up and finish this little job before dark," and he would start alongside me to keep me in countenance.

Many and many a time have the tears rolled down my cheeks as I saw other boys go off to bathe, or otherwise enjoy themselves, on the long summer evenings while my nose was held to the grindstone. On one occasion his kind-hearted wife observed my emotion, and remonstrated with him for not letting me off ; but he simply remarked that when he was a boy he had to work much harder than I did, which I daresay was true, at least in his estimation. The same good lady every morning at breakfast time used to send me out a slice of bread and butter at the hands of one of the children.

My work was almost entirely confined to painting the carts, ploughs, and other implements turned out from the workshop, for I was not yet considered sufficiently strong to handle the tools of the trade and work at the bench. An old sack, fastened upon me at the neck and waist, served for an apron and became so smeared with paint that it was as stiff as a board, and might be broken, but could not bend.

The clothes, which this protected, were overlaid with patches, some of which, on their getting loose, I used to fasten with nails instead of pins. Attired in such raiment, I was unable to walk about in public on Sundays ; but this was a privation for which I felt inwardly grateful, as it gave me the opportunity of spending that day lying reading under the shade of a tree in our garden.

Bad as I found my work in the summer, in the winter I found it still worse, for then we commenced at daylight in the morning and continued it till eight p.m., with one hour for dinner at four p.m. and breakfast before we started in the morning. On Friday nights we worked till eleven p.m., and this enabled us to get off on Saturday, our market day, at five p.m. Oh, how my heart used to rise at the approach of Saturday night, and how it sank at the approach of Monday morning ! " Sweet Saturday night and bitter Monday morning " was a saying I often heard quoted and always sympathised with. This feeling grew upon me to such a degree that I have never been able to shake it off, even when all my days became days of rest, and I still wake on Monday morning with uneasy feelings.

As I have already said, my passion for reading continued undiminished—I might even say intensified—and I used to gratify it in the early hours of the morning with the aid of my paraffin oil lamp. No book that I could beg, borrow, or even steal, if I had had the chance, came amiss to me. All printed matter bound in book form was acceptable, and if I could not get history, biography, poetry, or fiction, which, of course, were my favourites, I fell back on religious literature, just as a greedy boy might fall back on dry bread when the cakes and jam were all gone.

This religious literature was that which came oftenest in my way, for, in Cookstown, most of my neighbours who read anything at all would read nothing else, nor, in fact, allow any other sort into their houses. Perhaps I pay an undeserved compliment when I call it religious, for it was mainly sectarian and strongly imbued with the *odium theologicum* which permeates and poisons the atmosphere of Ulster. If I obtained Foxe's *Book of Martyrs* from some Protestant friend, I obtained Challoner's *Lives of the Missionary Priests* from a Catholic friend, and Chillingworth's *Religion of Protestants* was checkmated by Miliner's *End of Religious Controversy* ; the works of John Bunyan were weighed against those of Saint Alphonsus de Liguori, and the Six Days Controversy between Pope and Maguire made me an umpire between Catholic " Idolatry " and Protestant " Heresy." These sectarian discussions were rather common in the early days of the last century, and, conducted in public, were the begettors of much bitterness and bad blood. Each side would retire claiming victory over the other, but it is doubtful if either of them ever made a single convert by such discussions. In Ireland, unlike most other countries, a person's religion is not only a matter of conscience, but a matter of honour, and thus stands doubly fortified against all assaults from without.

The effect of all this polemical stuff on my mind was like that of two equal forces pulling in opposite directions with nil for resultant. Instead of drawing me to one side or the other, they compelled me to commune thus with myself : " A plague on both your houses, O ye graceless wielders of wind-bag weapons that make much noise and mean nothing."

In spite of this reflection, I passed for a good

Catholic, which my mother wished me to be, and to which honour constrained me in the presence of my employer and fellow-workmen, who were all oath-bound Orangemen. I remember on one occasion having a political discussion with my employer's brother, who, though an Orangemen, was neither illiterate nor unintelligent. I then stoutly maintained that the Irish were never conquered in fair, open fighting, but that the English had mastered them by sowing dissension amongst them, setting clan against clan and getting them to cut one another's throats. "That is probably quite true," was the purport, if not the words, of his reply, " and the English deserve all the more credit for this clever policy which made their work of conquest all the easier. If they found the Irish ready to cut one another's throats why should they not take advantage of it and save themselves from the trouble of doing it? If a foreign enemy landed in England, the English would not act in that way, but would prove themselves fit to own their country by uniting in its defence."

The truth of that remark fairly took the wind out of my argument, and I never again ventured to put it forth.

On another occasion, my religious principle, or, maybe, profession, was put to a crucial test. It happened thus : my employer and his men, including myself, went one day into the country with horses and carts to bring home some timber in the shape of fallen trees which he had bought from a farmer. The latter was a generous individual, and both able and willing to show his generosity in tangible form, so he brought us all into his house to have dinner. Though it was not unusual for me to feel hungry, I seemed to feel more hungry then than

I ever felt before, and as soon as I entered the house I inhaled the delicious smell of a roast goose that made my mouth water. But at the same time, it struck me like a flash of lightning that the day was _one_ of abstinence in the holy season of Advent, when Catholics were forbidden to eat flesh meat. What was I to do ? I reflected that if I partook of the goose, the pleasure of the meal would soon be over and leave me with an uneasy conscience that would ever afterwards degrade me in my own eyes by accusing me of moral cowardice and base desertion of my principle in presence of the enemy. So when the good farmer offered me a liberal helping, I refused it with thanks, and merely took a few potatoes flavoured with a pinch of salt.

The farmer looked at me with a smile that combined good nature and pity and remarked to the company :

" I suppose this lad keeps Friday, and if that's his principle he is quite right in sticking to it." They all assented, and they were all Orangemen, which enabled me to realise that the devil is never so black as he is painted. Knowing these men so well, I have never heard them being vilified without taking their part, so that once in Bristol at a meeting of my compatriots, I was saluted with the shout : " There's that bloody Orangeman from the North of Ireland ! "

We had many religious discussions, but always in a good-natured sort of way ; for, to their credit be it said, they never showed the slightest animosity to me on religious grounds, and invariably treated me not only with consideration but with courtesy and kindness ; and I have a very grateful recollection how one of them, named Rutherford, a nephew of

E

my employer, insisted on swapping boots with me, when mine were more than ordinarily bad, and pretended that he had the best of the bargain.

It was while working here that I acquired the uncanny reputation of being a master of the " Black Art "—a raiser of the Devil, a real disciple of " Harry Stotle " and " Cornelyus the Grupper." We had a black pig, which to my unspeakable disgust was housed in the warmest corner of our single living compartment, and though at first I detested the sight and smell of the unclean brute I gradually became reconciled to it, and at last friendly relations were established between us. I used to scratch and feed it, so that it took quite a fancy to me and would follow me like a pet dog.

Now, here was I in the eyes of our neighbours like no other human being, young in years, but old in appearance and still older in character, not taking the slightest interest in games of any sort and avoiding the companionship of boys and girls. When it was not work it was books, books all the time, and some of them, too, it was whispered, were " awfully deep." Of course, all these signs could point in only one direction—namely, that I had become a magician, had sold myself to the devil, and that his Satanic Majesty had sent one of his imps to attend me. It was told of one good man, who had been in America and was worthy of belief, that coming into our town on a certain night, at a late hour and by a lonely road, he heard something grunting behind him, and turning around saw " Mullin's black pig " pegging after him at an infernal rate. Though naturally a brave man, as he modestly admitted, he took to his heels and ran like blazes till he crossed Tullywiggan bridge, and then looking behind him the pig had disappeared, for, of course, it couldn't cross running water. I was told that mothers used to frighten their children by threatening to send for " Mullin's black pig."

These stories amused me immensely, for, although I looked such a solemn recluse, I am sure no person in our town could enjoy a joke more or was fonder of perpetrating one. I never boasted about my supernatural powers, but always affected to disparage them, but did it in such way that it impressed the listener far more than if I had boasted. If, for instance, a person said to me : " I don't believe a word of it." " Well, you're quite right. It's far better not to frighten yourself." And if I were asked if my pig would do him any harm I would reply : " No, I don't think he would, but it's better to be on the safe side and bless yourself every time you see him."

I had fine fun with a counterfeit half-crown which I coined from pewter. I would often in the presence of some garrulous acquaintance pull it out of my pocket and let him see it, as if by accident, and then in a tremulous hurry put it back as if I wished to hide it. He would say, " What's that you're hiding ? " and I would reply, " Oh, nothing in particular. I hope you didn't see it." " Yes, I saw it—it looked like a half-crown." " Well, since you saw it I must tell you the truth. That was the flying half-crown, but, for Heaven's sake, don't tell a livin' soul that you saw it with me or I'd lose my character entirely." " Oh, you may be sure an' sartin I won't," so off he would go to tell the first person he met, and next day everybody knew that young Mullin had " the flying half-crown."

Now, " the flying half-crown " is the coin for

which you sell yourself to the devil. Once you are in possession of that half-crown you can never get rid of it. You change it a hundred times a day— ten thousand times if you like—but when you leave the shop with a pennyworth of something and the change in your pocket, there is your precious half-crown amongst the change. In this way you can go home with a cartload of pennyworths and all your pockets bursting with change, both in silver and bronze.

The good people who ascribed the ownership of that coin to me never for a moment imagined that the very first use I would have put it to would be the purchase of a new suit of clothes and a daily supply of butcher's meat to fill out the said clothes.

When I was asked if I could raise the dead I said : Yes—only under certain conditions. If they wished to see a dead friend they would have to meet me at the graveside on any Friday at midnight, and then on their repeating the Devil's Litany three times in succession without drawing breath, I would introduce them to the lady or gentleman they wished to see. Needless to say, I was always spared the trouble of giving the introduction. In one case, however, I did perform my promise, not in raising a dead person, but in raising the devil himself. I was challenged by several young people to do so, and boldly accepted the challenge, named a certain night and a certain place for fulfilling it. In order to carry this out I had to take a fellow apprentice into my confidence, and this I did, at the same time instructing him in his part. On the appointed night my challengers assembled at the appointed place, and putting myself at their head I led them up a secluded bye-road, halting near a spot where it was bounded by a high hedge. I was armed with one of my largest books, and carried a hazel stick burned black at the end. It was hinted that this stick had been given to me by the devil, and that its blackened end was due to the fact that it had been used as a pencil in Hell for writing down the names of new-comers. When the right spot was reached, we halted, and I, grouping my companions closely together, drew on the ground around them a chalked circle, which, being white, no evil thing could enter, so I told them not to be afraid, but on no account to put a foot outside that circle. I then went on several yards farther, and, halting on the centre of the road, drew a black circle around myself with the burnt end of the hazel stick. This was followed by a loud rattling of chains on the other side, and I then shouted in a loud voice : " Mount Diabolus and fly," an expression which I had seen in Sir Walter's notes on the *Lay*. No sooner had I said these words than a flaming body flew up in the air, and no sooner did this come off than my audience, in spite of all my solemn injunctions, flew helter-skelter out of their white circle and left me alone in my glory. Not quite alone—for my accomplice joined me from the other side of the hedge, where I had planted him with a wisp of tow saturated with spirits of turpentine, which he ignited with a match and threw aloft at the psychological moment. We had a hearty laugh, but went home by different routes, and I don't think he ever split on me.

This last exploit put the finishing touch on my evil reputation, and the good people who formerly looked upon me with suspicion now looked upon me with horror. Some of the women-folk approached my mother about it, and implored her to burn all the books she could find in the house. At that time, unfortunately, her sight was failing, and she was unable to read the books, but naturally refused to burn them. However, to clear my character in the eyes of the neighbours she decided on bringing them to the parish priest to get the benefit of his judgment. Without telling me of this intention she carried it out in my absence ; but just then a lot of the books happened to be theological, and when the priest looked through them he told her she ought to thank Heaven she had such a religious son. The good man little knew that these books did not represent my choice, but my circumstances, and that they were not my delight but rather my disgust.

Although my character needed no clearing in the eyes of my mother, this action of hers cleared me considerably in the eyes of many people ; and they charitably considered that after all the Devil might not be so black as he is painted. As a matter of fact, he would really have been much blacker save for the exercise of more discretion than I ever gave myself the credit of possessing.

It happened thus. I was introduced by a mutual friend to a person called Pat Coy, who possessed an eighteenth century copy of *Paradise Lost* which I was most anxious to read, and I got it from him in return for the loan of an odd volume of Smith's *Panorama of the Arts and Sciences*. Now, if any man living was entitled to be called " handy " that man was my bold Pat. No work in metal came amiss to him ; he was locksmith, gunsmith, and tinsmith rolled into one, and could even clean old clocks. Above all, he was an expert coiner, and could make moulds from which he would turn out shillings, florins, and half-crowns as easily as you could shell peas. But although he was able to work all these wonders he was never able to keep himself, wife and children otherwise than half-starved and in rags ; in short, he could do anything except earn a decent living, and knew all the arts of success except the art of succeeding by commonsense and honesty. He initiated me into the mysteries of coining, and expatiated at great length on the fortune thereby obtainable. When I asked why he did not attain that fortune he replied that in order to do so he must have a partner to help him, and suggested that I should become that partner and share his fortune on condition that he should make the coins and that I should put them into circulation—a division of labour that would be entirely in my favour ! This suggestion filled me with no visions of a golden future, but it filled me with visions of a jail and myself inside and a heartbroken mother outside weeping. I then told my friend Pat that I would not blow into the muzzle of his gun while he played on the trigger.

After giving up all hope of getting me into partnership he secured another lad of about the same age, and called McVeigh. This lad was much sharper and handier than myself, so that he soon became as clever as his instructor, and after a brief but brilliant career managed to secure a long term of hospitality in Her Majesty's county hotel. After this Pat went to America, and I wished the Americans luck of their acquisition.

When two years of my apprenticeship had elapsed I was put to work at the bench, where I made such a poor show that I was put back to the painting. Just then a neighbour of ours, who was a timber merchant, and at the same time kept cartmaking and blacksmith works, offered to take me into his employment at three shillings a week. This offer was too tempting to be resisted, so I closed upon it immediately and left my first master without a moment's notice. I don't think he was in the least put out over it, nay, rather I think he was glad to get rid of such a bad bargain as I promised to be. Years afterwards when I told him it was a lucky day for him when I left him : " Aye," said he, " but it was a far luckier day for yourself." He was a hard master, but I always entertained the highest respect for him, and if he died a comparatively wealthy man, every penny of his wealth was the result of hard work and honest.

During all the time I had been in his employment I had no money to spend on books beyond a few pence which I sometimes received as a present from my master and sometimes from his customers. If I attempted to retain even a penny from my weekly half-crown my mother would not take the remainder but would tell me to go somewhere else for my food during the week, for she could not afford to provide me with it ; and sure enough no food would be cooked in our house till I had forked out the last farthing. On such occasions she would ask me with sardonic humour : " Why don't you go to the hotel for your meals ? "

Being thus at my wits' end to obtain books, I decided on a course that would render few books necessary, at least for the time being, and at the same time give me mental employment. This decision was to learn the Latin and Greek languages, for which all I wanted would be a couple of grammars to start with. I managed by some means to get an old copy of *Ruddiman's Rudiments of Latin Grammar*, but a Greek grammar was beyond my reach just then,

I had long before felt impelled to take this course
from the inspiration of an old book in two volumes
which I had managed to pick up in the local pawn-
shop. It was the lives of the principal Greek and
Roman Poets and Historians, and in addition to their
lives described their works in the most glowing
terms. That book charmed me as few books have
ever done. But then it was written by " A Gentleman," and, of course, the best might be expected;
and my expectation at least was not disappointed.
This book became one of my chief favourites and
inflamed me with the desire of mastering the treasures
it described, and so I embarked on *Ruddiman's
Rudiments*.

I pursued the task rather intermittently at first,
always interrupting it when a fresh book came in my
way. And fresh books did come in my way through
a fine stroke of luck that interrupted my Latin lessons
for three months. It came about in this way. In
a shop in our town, kept by the Misses McCormick,
two dear elderly ladies, very like those that figure in
Cranford, I used to peep through the window at
books that were littered on the sill inside. Very fine
books they were, too, which I would have given
worlds to read. Having decided to try whether
they might be within my reach, I entered the shop
and inquired if the books were for sale. No, they
were not for sale, as I knew quite well, they belonged
to the Cookstown Library located there, and with its
well-filled shelves occupying one side of the shop.
They had been purchased by surplus funds of the
local Loan Bank and were intended for the use of the
better-class readers—respectable shopkeepers, bank
clerks, parsons, etc., etc.

The subscription was five shillings a year, and the

person to receive subscriptions was a Mr. Stark, Manager to the local branch of the Ulster Bank. Now, five shillings was an impossible sum for me to raise, but I might raise fifteen pence for a quarter's subscription, and after a few weeks' scraping together of casual coppers, I succeeded in amassing this sum, and with it approached the treasurer, who in my eyes seemed a most important personage. To my great disappointment he refused to accept it, stating that no less than a year's subscription could be received. I turned away with a heavy heart and a distressed look, when he called me back and told me he would make an exception to the rule in my case, and forthwith supplied me with a card for a quarter's reading, accompanied with a friendly caution to take great care of the books. I handled that card with a rapture which a passport to Paradise could hardly have given. The old lady librarian was very much astonished when I, only a working lad in working clothes, presented the card, and was still more astonished at my discrimination in the selections made.

The library contained the cream of Victorian literature, which, being then copyright, had been far beyond my reach; and into it I plunged with as much avidity as a gold-digger would plunge into a new mine overflowing with the richest ore. I sampled the very foremost authors only—amongst historians, Hallam, Macaulay, Prescott, and Motley; Tennyson and Browning amongst poets, and Dickens and Thackeray amongst novelists; and I wound up the quarter with Boswell's *Johnson*, which, unfortunately, I had not time to finish.

The dark and dismal winter had then set in, and the long night-work it entailed reduced my time for reading to the merest minimum, and I calculated that if I paid for another quarter I should not get value for my fifteenpence, and so I resumed my Latin grammar. It was, I believe, in the summer following that I again applied for admission to the library with another quarter's subscription, and this was again refused, but on far different grounds. I was then informed, to my great surprise, and still greater delight, that I need pay no more subscriptions, for it had been decided that I should have the free use of the library as long as I chose and without conditions. Long afterwards I learned that this proposal was made and financed by the master of the local Academy, Mr. Samuel James McMullan, M.A., Gold Medallist of the Queen's University, and subsequently Professor of English Literature in Queen's College, Belfast. He was quite unknown to me except by appearance, and I never had an opportunity of expressing my deep gratitude to him, for he left our town long before I knew he was my benefactor. He has long since passed away, but his reputation for goodness of heart and greatness of ability still lives in the memory of all who had the pleasure of knowing him. I took full advantage of his kindly act, and continued to borrow from the library till I practically exhausted all the best literature it contained ; and the reason why its literature was so good was because my benefactor himself had selected it.

After this I reverted to Latin, but in the meantime some changes had befallen me. In the new job I had taken on, the conditions were better in respect of wages, regularity of working hours, and the reduced rate at which I was driven ; but they were worse in the exchange of kindly, obliging, and helpful workmates for one who showed the reverse of all these qualities. As my employer himself did not work, and, in fact, seldom came into the workshop, I was at the mercy of a foreman who both directly and indirectly did all he could to make my position unbearable and drive me out of it. He was sulky, sullen, and ill-natured, and when his tongue did find freedom it was only to indulge in jeers and taunts. Whatever piece of work I got to do would be impeded by obstacles placed in my way by his contrivance. He was, however, an excellent workman, finishing to perfection every job he undertook. By watching him carefully without pretending to do so, I picked up a lot of his skill, especially in the art of wheelmaking, and when I left at the end of eight months I was as good a workman as himself, at least in that branch of my trade.

I was then about eighteen, and was offered work at five shillings a week by another carpenter, and closed on the offer without losing a day. In this place I remained four years, and very miserable years they were, even though my pay was rising, and the light was beginning to break on my career. There were three apprentices in the shop, and I, save the mark, was foreman. The master himself, occasionally, did some work, and when he did so his presence was a terror amongst us. He had a vile temper, which he cultivated for all it was worth at the expense of myself and the apprentices. By turns he would bully and browbeat us, and by turns he would ply us with sarcastic jokes and would rarely leave us in peace. With myself he was much disappointed, and, indeed, I could hardly blame him, for I was an awfully slow coach, and although all my work was exceedingly well done, it would probably take me four days to finish a job which a smart workman would finish in three. Quantity and not quality was the rule to which I could not comply, try as I would. This, however, was not my fault but my misfortune, for my strength was far below the average workman's, and so was my feeding, but all the same I was expected to do at least the average amount of work.

When my employer had taken more drink than was good for him, a contingency which often occurred, he showed the temper of a demon, and in these paroxysms I have seen him pursue his apprentices with a stick. I am a firm believer in the Horatian maxim : " *In vino veritas*," and consider that drink does not put the devil into a man, but by paralysing the controlling power of the brain it lets loose the devil that lurks in a man's character. And if no devil lurks there, it opens the floodgates of good nature and geniality, so that every man, good or bad, is shown in his true colours when under the influence of drink. But in his most violent fits of temper, this man would suddenly become quite calm and amiable on taking " a draw of the pipe," as taking a smoke was called amongst us. I really never saw such a transformation. In spite of his temper I cannot say I disliked him, for he had a warm heart, and was always willing to do a good turn if it lay in his power, and I hold his memory in kindly regard. He had a son whom I have tried to remember with the same feeling, but must confess I have found it hard to do so.

This young man's temper was quite unlike his father's ; it was a freezing mixture, compounded of arrogance, sarcasm, and conceit that penetrated to the marrow. His overmastering vanity cheated him into the belief that he was one of the "smartest" of men living, and he would use the biggest words on the smallest matters, especially in my presence, in order to impress me with a proper sense of his importance and my own insignificance. One day as I passed him painting a dogcart he stopped me, and, striking an attitude, said : "Sir, I would not exchange my profession for a collegiate career." Although I had no prospect of a "collegiate career" at that time I took the remark as an impertinent slight flung at my bookish propensity. He always alluded to me as "the poet" by way of a taunt, and I always alluded to him as "the snob." It would be difficult to decide which of us showed the greater contempt for the other. He, however, had the whip hand of me, for he was much older and stronger, and a much smarter workman, on which point I was being continually taunted. As I was then morbidly sensitive and prone to exaggerate the slightest disparagement into the deadliest insult, this everlasting nagging galled me dreadfully and often drew deep sighs from me as I sat at my meals.

I should, of course, have left this place without a moment's notice, but no other in our town was open for me, and I could not think of leaving my mother, now old, infirm, and almost blind. She was not, however, blind to my distress, but felt it as keenly as I myself did, and then proceeded to rouse me up with her advice, wholesome and bracing as usual.

Why should I allow these people to make little of me when the remedy was in my own hands ? It was because I worked too cheaply that they put so little value on me and my work. She did not think I had the pluck to stand up against them, so she herself would face them at the end of the week and demand that my pay must be doubled, and if they refused I must leave them and look for work somewhere else. I was not to think of her, for she was more troubled to see me unhappy than she would be to live alone.

It was impossible for me not to admire her views and agree with them; and so on the following Saturday night she went to my employer's house and demanded that my pay should be advanced to ten shillings, but was met with the reply that I was getting as much as I was worth, and never in the whole course of my life should I be able to earn ten shillings a week. If we were not satisfied with five I might go to Hell. Well, I did not go there, but I went on strike and stuck to it till my employer caved in with a very bad grace. With the increase of pay my position became utterly unbearable. I was expected to do more and more work, which was quite impossible, as my power had been already taxed to the very uttermost; so after a few weeks I left without giving a word of notice. In doing so I gave them reason to consider that I had treated them as unfairly as I considered they had treated me.

CHAPTER IV

With my departure from my second place the pathway of my existence, that seemed so monotonous, dreary, and unpromising, took a slight turn for the better, and a glimmer of light began to penetrate the gloom that overshadowed it.

But I must revert to certain events that occurred to me whilst I trudged through this *via crucis* of four years duration. One was an incident which religious-minded people would call providential and worldly-minded people a " lucky accident." It happened thus : One Saturday morning I was going from my work to breakfast when my eye lit on a dirty-looking piece of paper lying folded up on the footpath. I picked it up and to my unspeakable delight found it was a one pound note. I kept it clenched in my fist, not risking to pocket it, until I got home, when I carefully hid it in the roof behind a rafter, never mentioning it to a living soul. At that time I had reverted to my Latin studies, but had no books with the exception of *Ruddiman's Rudiments* and *Swain's Sentences*. And now here was I, O joy of joys ! the possessor of means to purchase whatever books I wanted.

On Easter Monday, which followed soon after, I went on a cheap trip to Belfast and purchased at second-hand *Ainsworth's Latin Dictionary*, *Anthon's Sallust*, and the *Edinburgh Greek Grammar*, also new copies of *Anthon's Virgil* and *Cæsar's Commentaries*. I returned home with these treasures in a transport of delight, like another Jason returning with a golden fleece. Through Cæsar's *De Bello Gallico* I waltzed much more easily than I expected ; through the first two books of the *Æneid* with much pleasure, but I fairly stuck at the opening sentence of Sallust's *Catiline*. I happened, however, to know a teacher who had been educated for the priesthood, and, baiting him with the prospect of getting a pupil, I enticed him to construe the sentence for me. For this purpose I walked to his residence seven miles off, and considered the walk well rewarded. With my subsequent Latin I experienced little or no difficulties.

About the same time I began to be recognised amongst the most intellectual of my fellow-townsmen. They had started a society for the discussion of literary and scientific subjects, and I was unanimously elected a member. I was very proud of the honour, for I was the only workingman to whom it had been given, and it gave me a great lift over my employer's son, who showed that he felt it keenly. This society consisted of clerks, shopkeepers, schoolmasters, medical and clerical students—in fact, all the young men of the locality who had any pretence to literary or scientific culture or felt a desire for improvement. Many things have faded away from my memory, but their friendship will remain green while life lasts.

The meetings of our society were held in the Courthouse every Wednesday at eight p.m., and I, in order to get off from my work in due time, sacrificed the dinner hour, and as I had breakfast before starting at eight a.m., I thus worked without food for about eleven hours. Debates, essays, and public readings constituted the business of the meetings, and

F

were always purely academic on literary and historical subjects—the hackneyed subjects of debating societies. " Was Cæsar a greater general than Hannibal ? " was a debate in which I figured on the negative side ; and " Was Grattan a greater orator than Curran ? " when I figured on the affirmative side, and it made me insufferably vain to find myself on the victorious side each time.

I took part in all the discussions and criticisms, never hiding my light under a bushel, and dragged in all manner of allusions to show off my erudition. I even had the audacity to write an essay on the Greek Classics, giving as samples Homer, Pindar, Herodotus, and Thucydides. For this purpose I used without scruple my copy of the *Classic Biography* written by " A Gentleman," to which I have already referred. This brought me into conflict with a fellow-member called Mooney, a Greek scholar studying for the priesthood, who took up the Wolfian theory that the Homer of tradition had no more existence than Sairey Gamp's friend, Mrs. Harris. I took up the cudgel on the orthodox side, and the controversy waxed hot and furious, more to the amusement than instruction of the members. My doughty adversary is now a Trappist in the monastery of Mount Melleray in Ireland, and honoured me with a visit a couple of years ago when we had a hearty laugh over that controversy.

He then told me a somewhat pathetic story of himself. After being in the monastery fourteen years he happened to visit Cork. On his going into a restaurant for lunch an old man in clerical garb, with bent back and grey hair, came forward meeting him, and both raised their hats to each other at the same time. What was his astonishment to find that

the old gentleman was his own reflection in a huge
mirror that filled the opposite end of the hall. For
fourteen years he had not looked into a mirror, and
his appearance had so changed during that time that
he failed to recognise it !

The biggest score I made in the Association was
a poetical essay called " Genius," written in ten-
syllable rhyming couplets, so fashionable in the
eighteenth century, and which could be rolled out
in reams far easier than respectable prose. Although
my production was as flat as anything turned out in
the time of William or Anne, it passed muster for
poetry amongst the members of our Association,
and by a unanimous vote they decided to have it
printed, published, and sold for sixpence a copy.
How many copies were sold I do not know, but I
know it never reached a second edition, and no copy
of it ever came into my possession.

Our Association was in every way an unqualified
benefit to its members, and indirectly to the community in general. It drew together young men of
the most opposite opinions in religion and politics,
and by leading them to an interchange of ideas on
literary, historical, and sociological questions enabled
them to treat one another with a respect that laid
the foundations of future friendship. Politics and
religion were wisely excluded from our debates, for
they would have driven us into opposite camps
where each of us should have felt bound in honour
to fight for the principles of his own side, held as
sacrosanct, against the principles of the other side,
held as damnable.

It was the means of letting the Protestant realise
that his Catholic neighbour was not so ignorant and
inferior as perhaps he had been taught to believe ;

and it led the Catholic to realise that his Protestant neighbour was not such a bigoted and arrogant ruffian as he was represented.   It was a plank in that platform of Reconciliation on which the future weal of Ireland must stand.

There are other societies to-day in Ireland conducted on other lines, where " mutual improvement " consists in keeping open the gulf of prejudice that has kept our people apart for centuries.   But as the new dawn breaks upon Ireland these centres of darkness will surely disappear.

I should have said that long before joining this Society I was connected with another, which, though neither literary nor scientific, was none the less interesting.   This was the Fenian Association, with which I became connected some time in '65, when it was making great headway in Ireland about the close of the American Civil War.   I was very proud and pleased to join the movement, for I had always been an enthusiastic Nationalist, and one of my dearest ambitions was to strike a blow for making " Ireland a Nation."   I had been indoctrinated into republicanism by my mother, who impressed me with the meanness of bowing the head and bending the knee to any man or set of men made from the same clay as myself and set above me by accident only. This creed was confirmed by an early perusal of Paine's *Rights of Man*, and though modified by time has never been shaken.

I am sure my Nationalism must have been an inherited instinct, for I cannot remember its beginning ; and as soon as I could read I took most delight in reading books and papers that glorified Ireland to the disparagement of the Predominant Partner.

I was not taught to cultivate such a feeling, nor did I ever hear it expressed amongst those with whom I mixed, so that it must have been transmitted from rebel ancestors. My mother, indeed, used to speak of a relative of hers named Logue who was one of the " United Men " of '98. This poor man was captured by the Royalists, and in order to make him inform on his comrades, who were in hiding, his captors took him to a place called the Gallows Hill, near Magherafelt, South Derry, and there they enclosed him in a barrel with nails pointed inwards and rolled him down the hill. At the bottom he was taken out and flogged, and with each stroke of the lash was asked if he would inform, and each time he replied : " Never till death." In the end they let him off alive, but so badly punished that his reason gave way, and though he lived for some years afterwards he kept continually muttering, " Never till death."

This story was neither told in a spirit of vindictiveness, nor intended to stimulate my national sentiments ; for such sentiment in those days, the fifties, when I first heard it, was almost extinct in Ireland, which Gavan Duffy, as he left the country, pronounced to be as dead as a corpse on the dissecting table. As far as I can remember, everything National was rigorously tabooed amongst the middle classes, especially shopkeepers ; and it would make angels blush and the devil laugh to observe their attempts at cultivating an English accent. Under such circumstances my Nationalism came from within, not from without.

Amongst my other reading I had dipped into Irish history, and had acquired an intimate knowledge of all the best Anglo-Irish literature, both in prose and verse. My favourite poets were Davis and Mangan, and my favourite prose writer was John Mitchel—a writer as forcible as Swift and as picturesque as Carlyle. Under such inspiration I was led to detest O'Connell's degrading doctrine that a nation's freedom is not worth one drop of blood, and I became an enthusiastic supporter of the doctrine that no nation is worthy of freedom who is not willing to shed blood in winning it. This was the doctrine of Fenianism—a doctrine that put new life into the corpse on the dissecting table.

When the movement spread to our town I became one of the first recruits, the oath of admission being administered by the head centre, or Captain of the district. That oath ran as follows : " I (repeating my name) do hereby swear allegiance to the Irish Republic now virtually established. That I will take up arms at a moment's notice to defend its independence and integrity, and will obey the commands of my superior officers in all things not contrary to the laws of God. So help me God." As the Fenians were, and probably still are, looked upon as a secret society, and as such were banned by Catholic bishops, if not by the Catholic Church, it is noteworthy that there is no mention of secrecy in their oath. Not only were they well-known, but they gloried in the fact, and advertised it by affecting a military strut. The only thing mysterious about them was their name.

Invested with the glamour of antiquity, this name was a very catchy one, and owed its adoption to John O'Mahony, an eminent Irish scholar domiciled in New York. Originally it was the name given to the Irish Militia, or National Guards, who flourished some centuries before the Christian era under the leadership of that renowned chieftain, Fionn, the father of Ossian.

The Fenians of my day were a military body, if a number of young men without arms or equipment could be called such. They had no drill except what they could pick up by night, owing to the stringency of the Illegal Training and Drilling Act; and on such occasions their drill instructors were militiamen. If, however, they had neither arms nor training, they had plenty of enthusiasm, if enthusiasm could be measured by songs and speeches in the back parlours of publichouses. Their ideals were the loftiest of the lofty, their means of action the poorest of the poor. Never since the Knight of the Rueful Countenance set forth with sword and spear to redress all the wrongs of mankind, was there such an ill-assorted combination. Nowadays it is difficult outside of Ireland to imagine any body of sane men obsessed with the idea of defeating the British Army, horse, foot, and artillery, with no other weapons than those which Nature had provided them with in the shape of their fists and feet, and such others as Providence might drop from the skies. To all but themselves they seem like a parcel of boys armed with popguns going out in a small rowing boat to fight a super-dreadnought. Yet such men existed in '65 and '67, and unfortunately exist still, with less reason, and it strikes me as one of Fate's funniest ironies that I was one of them. Yet I feel no regret for it, and under similar circumstances should probably be the same again.

It is true we were told by a sympathetic priest, who was a *rara avis* amongst his brethren, that an Irishman fighting for his country was a match any day for two redcoats armed only with rifles and bayonets, and fighting for a shilling a day. The wisdom of this opinion raised the speaker so high in my estimation that I felt if I were the Irishman placed in such an advantageous position I should be strongly tempted to relinquish it in the good man's favour, hand him my cudgel, and unselfishly allow him to carry off the honours of victory.

A gun club was started to which every member subscribed a few pence weekly, and in return for same was promised a rifle and bayonet in due time. I became a member, and for a few weeks subscribed a few pence towards the purchase of a pike and revolver, weapons which would bring me into closer contact with the enemy and thereby ensure us a speedier victory. Fortunately, however, for the enemy, these weapons were not put into my hands, nor did I see any prospect of such being the case; so I stopped subscribing for them and contented myself with the reflection that when the rising occurred I would supply myself with arms at the expense of somebody else, bethinking me of Virgil's " *Furor arma ministrat.*"

Our drillings, as I have said, took place by night, but one Sunday we had a grand field-day in a mountainous district some ten miles off where the inhabitants were all on our side; and we spent the livelong day in marching, countermarching, forming fours, and preparing to resist cavalry. But whilst thus mindful of our duty as patriots we were no less mindful of our duty as Catholics, and so, before commencing the serious business of the day, we attended Mass in the local chapel. The good priest soon spotted us and poured on our devoted heads a torrent of abuse that was neither lukewarm nor stinted; and if Hell did not open and swallow us there and then I am sure it was not his fault. We retaliated by rising and leaving the chapel in a body, and he then exhorted his congregation to give us " the cold shoulder and the hot foot;" in short, to run away from us. For acting thus he subsequently received the thanks of the local gentry, and the silent contempt of his own young people.

Our bitterest enemies were not the government authorities, but the ecclesiastical authorities, both bishops and priests. All Ireland rang with their denunciations delivered publicly from their altars and privately in our own houses. One worthy bishop, Moriarty of Kerry, proclaimed that Hell was not hot enough nor eternity long enough to punish us. If their motives were excellent, the methods of the clericals were execrable, conducted as they were with all the arrogance, bluster, and browbeating for which their worst enemies give them credit—a policy that defeated its object. If they had expostulated with us in a friendly or even in a reasonable manner, sympathising with our motives as being honourable and patriotic, but at the same time only possible to lead to bloodshed and irretrievable disaster, they might have diverted a good many of us from the path of danger. But no—they used taunts, jibes, and insults, and seemed absolutely astounded that their dictatorship in the domain of politics should be called in question. This attitude put us on our mettle ; we met it with contempt and defied their power.

Never since Pope Adrian sold the country to an English king for the promise of Peter's pence was that power in a more parlous position in Ireland, nor Reason more militant. We had a weekly paper, called *The Irish People*, and this paper paid off the clericals in their own coin. Every week it had a column headed "Priests, Peelers, and Magistrates"[1] in which the priests were nicknamed the "Black-Coated Traitors," "The Maynooth Lawyers" and "John Bull's Beef-Eaters," in allusion to the Maynooth grant which their students then enjoyed. They waged war against this paper with all the virulence which only self-conscious rectitude is able to engender. It was their custom to make house-to-house visitations to find where the paper was harboured, and if perchance they spied a copy it was reported that they would seize it with the tongs and commit it to the fire without condescending to touch it, just as the Holy Office might deal with a heretic.

All the newsagents over whom they had any influence were forbidden to sell it ; but in such cases the boys, as in our town, would get parcels of it and hawk them around on Saturday nights, in which work I took an active part. Not only did I assist it in this way, but my vanity prompted me to write verses for it, some of which appeared over my initials, and others were relegated to the everlasting limbo of the waste-paper basket. I remember one piece headed " Ode to the Pike," on which an extinguisher was put with the editorial remark : " We hope J. M. can handle the Pike better than the Pen " !

I was one of the first to attract clerical notice, and the curate requested, or rather ordered, me to sever my connection with the movement. On receiving a negative that must have staggered his self-importance, he proceeded to tell me that I was

---

[1] Time works out his revenges ! Who would have thought that the arch-purloiner of principles would have destined myself to figure in one of these odious groups ?

in a state of " final reprobation," which meant, I
suppose, that I was inevitably booked through to
Hades ; and added that if I were dying no priest
in Ireland would lay hands on me. I thanked him
for the compliment, and turned my back upon him
with a smile which I might bestow on a dog whose
bark was furious, but whose jaws were toothless
This gentleman became a high dignitary of the
Catholic Church in Ireland, and I hope that the
years which brought him so much honour also
brought him a little charity. I am afraid that I
filled a very unhallowed niche in his memory, for
some years afterwards when I was a university
graduate and attended a Mass in my native town
where he officiated, his eye fell on me as he entered
the pulpit, with the result that his congregation was
treated to a scathing sermon on the evils of a godless
education—the very last thing in the world against
which the poor souls needed warning.

Our paper, *The Irish People*, which had so long
withstood the thunder of the Church, succumbed at
last to the thunder of Dublin Castle, and its entire
staff, editor, manager, and printer, were arrested.
This blow was soon followed by another one, namely,
the suspension of the Habeas Corpus Act, which
meant that any person could be arrested and kept in
prison without trial as long as the authorities wished.

Under the new dispensation three of my comrades
were arrested, the most prominent of them being
my employer's son. Several others sought safety
in exile, and an end was put to the drilling.

Everybody said that young Mullin was sure to be
the next arrested, but though I well deserved that
honour it was not my luck to obtain it. I kept on
at my work as if nothing had happened, but I took
the precaution of leaving home every night and

sleeping at the house of my aunt, two miles away. I did this because all the arrests were made at night, or rather in the early hours of the morning. In approaching our house each morning, I looked out for a signal arranged to be made in case an unwelcome visit had been paid. This signal I could see at a distance without exposing myself. It was never shown—much to my disgust—for it humiliated me to reflect that after all I might not be such a dangerous enemy to the government as I imagined. I felt just as Tom Steele might have felt, had he missed the honour of getting arrested with his leader, O'Connell. "Look here, Tom," said the Chief Secretary, "if you don't stop worrying me about it, by G—d I won't have you arrested after all."

It might be imagined that at this time my mother would be in a terrible state of anxiety about the danger into which I was drifting, but contrary to my expectation and much to my delighted surprise her attitude was one of friendly neutrality. While she did not openly encourage me in my risky conduct, she did so indirectly by the praise she showered on the brave men who were prepared to lay down their lives for their country, and the odium she heaped on the skulkers who preferred personal safety to patriotic duty. In this opinion she was the faithful type of her countrywomen both then and now. Being a born fighter, she often castigated me for not showing enough of the same spirit.

She told me with the highest admiration of a woman whom she knew in her early days, like herself a widow and the mother of an only son, who had been challenged to fight a rival. The mother, so far from trying to prevent the fight, gave him every encouragement, and on the morning of the encounter sent him forth with the following useful tip : " Be sure to give him the first *polthogue* on the butt of the lug, an' then keep hammerin' away at the same spot, but for the love o' God don't waste your blows spreadin' them all over the baste's body." Encouraged in this way he returned victorious, but probably would have returned vanquished had the mother tried to restrain him with tears and entreaties. From this I learned how I might expect to be sent forth to battle and how I might be expected to return.

Although a notice was circulated that we should commence open hostilities in a fortnight, the notice expired without an effort to fulfil it ; and the whole movement gradually collapsed after a few abortive risings in the south. As these took place outside my personal ken, I feel they are equally outside my personal narrative.

Although Fenianism thus fizzled out, it must not be assumed that it did so without results ; indeed, no rebellion in Ireland ever passed away without issue ; but this movement was more fruitful than any previous one, and no other bore results that were more beneficial to the country. It put a spirit into the people that enabled them to overthrow clerical dictatorship in the domain of politics, and emboldened them to sympathise with every move- ment for freedom, no matter what power it was aimed against or by what power it was started. For a narrow sectarianism it sought to substitute a faith that would embrace all creeds in a brotherhood of patriotism working for the welfare of a common country. It encouraged the helots of centuries to cast aside their self-abasement and raise their heads as equals amongst the free people of the world. It shattered their superstitious belief in the divine right of kings and the arrogant pretensions of a hereditary aristocracy. It sowed the seeds of the Land League and the National League, which ripened into the two-fold harvest of the Land Acts and the Home Rule Acts. Nay more, it enriched Ireland's bead-roll of patriots with names that any country might be proud of—names which Englishmen themselves would honour if they were Italian or Polish. My connection with such a movement is not a matter to be ashamed of; it causes me no regret and needs no apology.

Another result of the Fenian movement was to confirm an observation first made, I believe, by Lucian, to the effect that Apollo and the Muses always favour the losing side—an observation of which even our own history affords many notable instances, especially in connection with the Jacobite risings and the Irish rebellions, where the very finest ballad literature was produced by the losing sides and nothing but a few wretched doggerel rhymes by the winner. The ballads and lyrics of the '48 and of the Fenian movements comprise the finest gems in Anglo-Irish literature; so that after all it may somewhat console those whose ancestors were defeated in the domain of brute force, to know that they were victors in the domain of intellect, wherein the fruits of victory are the more lasting.

Although the *Sinn Féin* movement of our own day has produced a large amount of verse, all its leading spirits being poets more or less, I question whether it will stand the same chance of survival as its predecessors. As far as I can make out it has less grip in it, is too fine-spun and wraith-like. Its voice sounds like autumnal winds moaning through leafless woods, and, much as it may be affected by the dilettante, will never touch the people's heart.

I often smile at the irony of Fate which has made a staunch supporter of the British Connection out of such an uncompromising rebel as I considered myself. But I attribute this fact to the changed attitude of the British people, my better knowledge of their character, and my complete confidence in their sense of justice.

When *The Irish People* was suppressed I transferred my allegiance and subscription to another paper called *The Irishman*, which picked up the national flag and seemed to keep it flying in the face of difficulty and danger. Its war-whoop was almost as vigorous as that of its predecessor, and I fondly believed that my prophet's mantle fell on no unworthy shoulders. Its proprietor, manager, and editor, was Richard Pigott, who afterwards earned an immortality of infamy.

As no newsagent in our district could be got to sell the paper through the fear of a Government prosecution I wrote to Pigott to send me my copy direct from his office in Dublin. The result was that he sent me some two dozen copies, exhorting me to sell them at a profit of twenty-five per cent. I did so, and then he kept sending more and more till its circulation in our neighbourhood at least doubled ; and every Saturday night our house was visited by many purchasers and became a well-known Nationalist rendezvous. Pigott then sent me another publication called *The Shamrock*, for which I also obtained many purchasers. I regret to say that a large proportion of my clientèle paid me with promises instead of pence, so that after a time I gave up the business—a sadder but not a richer man.

I had several letters from Pigott which I did not preserve, as I should have done could I have guessed his subsequent career.   The only thing I remember about them is the pious tone in which they were couched.

CHAPTER V

I continued to work at my trade with the same employer until his son was liberated from prison and for some considerable time afterwards ; but although I worked as hard as my strength would allow and did my level best to keep the business afloat, I received no consideration, much less gratitude, and was subject to a continual nagging and grumbling that made my life unbearable and decided me on leaving, come what might. Accordingly I did so on a Saturday night without giving a moment's notice, but with my mother's approval. On the following Monday morning, I started on tramp, heading in the direction of Belfast, and determined to take the first job that might be offered in the first workshop I turned into.

My impedimenta on this expedition consisted of the working clothes I wore, together with a carpenter's two-foot rule in my trousers pocket and the Edinburgh Greek Grammar in my jacket pocket. I calculated on being some considerable time without books and that the contents of this little book would quite suffice for my spare moments during that time.

I tramped to the town of Magherafelt, nine miles off on the high-road to Belfast, and was lucky enough to get engaged in the very first workshop I entered. I was to receive five shillings a week with board and lodging, and my work consisted in making and mending cart-wheels, with occasional bouts of coffin-making for the local workhouse—my employer being

G

contractor for the latter work. There must have been an awful mortality in that workhouse, for we often sent them a cartload of coffins of the roughest workmanship and painted black with a decoction of lamp-black, burnt straw, and water. He afterwards lost that contract, for some of the guardians complained that they could see the faces of the corpses through the joints of the coffin lids.

My employer's name was Davy Steenson, a lame old man whose working days were over, though he still superintended. My heart warmed to him, for he was good-natured and placid, and seldom appeared without a pipe in his mouth, which I always consider a good sign, and, without being able to imitate, envy those who can enjoy it. My fellow-workman was Dennis O'Neill, one of the most perfervid Catholics I ever met. He always spoke of Protestants as " the unbaptised heretics," and was never funny except when he was deadly serious. Like many bigots of both sects whom I have known, Dennis was not to be measured by his words, and though sanguinary in his language, was really good-natured and would not hurt a worm even though he knew it to be an unbaptised heretic.

I got on very well in this employment and liked my master and his family immensely, and having earned the reputation of being a good workman was treated with more deference than I had been accustomed to. This liking, however, did not extend to my lodgings, for as there was no bedroom for me in my employer's house I was sent to a lodging-house outside. I would call it a common lodging-house, but I dare not; for in comfort, cleanliness, and hygiene it was as far below a common lodging-house as the latter is below a first-class hotel.

It consisted of a large kitchen with a loft reached by a ladder, and in this loft all the lodgers slept, each one paying twopence a night. It contained two wooden bedsteads, one of which was occupied by a tinker, his wife, and three children, and the other by myself and any casual tramp that happened to turn up. But the floor was littered with half-a-dozen straw mattresses, each of which had its occupant every night, and on the market night, Thursday, generally two occupants. There was no ventilation except by the manhole through which we made our exits and entrances, and there was no light except through a small skylight in the roof. The stench was unbearable except to well-seasoned noses, and the heat during the summer nights was like that of an oven. I used to get up by daybreak, and on looking around beheld a sight that would have sent Mrs. Grundy into fits. All the lodgers lay fast asleep, and most of them as naked as when they first entered the world, for what with the heat and irritation caused by the persistent attacks of those slow-moving but ferocious invaders familiarly known amongst us as the " Scotch Greys," they had kicked off the old bed coverings and lay *puris naturalibus*, like skinned rabbits.

But what, it may be asked, about the nightshirts ? Well, I doubt if these articles of apparel were known amongst them even by name, and their day-clothes rolled up in bundles, were kept away from their beds as far as possible—a very wise precaution which hard experience compelled them to adopt. This habit of sleeping naked, repellent as it seems to our conventional notions of decency, I afterwards found to be quite common amongst the Italian peasantry, and is not without its advantages. On hot nights when sleep is found to be impossible and every turn in the bed intensifies the irritability of the peripheral nerve endings, it is pleasant to throw off the clothes that cling so exasperatingly to the skin, and allow a current of fresh air to circulate around the teased, tormented, and excoriated membrane. Sometimes this treatment for sleeplessness has to be supplemented by a cold sponge bath, which seldom fails of the desired effect. On a visit to Tripoli, in Barbary, during the sirocco, it worked like a charm in my own case. My attention was first drawn to it in the writings of Benjamin Franklin.

On market nights, when the loft would be packed with " dossers," it was quite a treat to listen to their conversations, even when one paid sleepless hours for it. These conversations would always turn on exploits that redounded to the credit and illustrated the cleverness of the speaker. I remember one rag and bone gatherer, known as " Scroggy," boasting of his day's work in tricking a farmer's wife out of ten shillings' worth of feathers. He had happened to get possession of a brand-new farthing glittering like real gold, and armed with this he boldly entered the farmhouse to purchase feathers. All the family were off in the market except the goodwife herself, and, as good luck would have it, she had some feathers to sell, for which she wanted ten shillings. " Scroggy " looked at the feathers and agreed to purchase them at the price, and handing her the farthing told her to change " the sovereign " and keep ten shillings. The good woman regretted that she could not change it as there was no money in the house. Looking as generous as his villainous features would allow he told her that he considered her a " dacent, honest woman," and so he would allow her to keep the

" sovereign " until he would come round again " in the coorse iv a week," and by that time maybe she would have another ten shillings' worth ready for him, and so he wouldn't trouble for the change at all, at all. She then wrapped up the " sovereign " in an old stocking and carefully stowed it away under the bed-tick. This and many other stories like it were told with such gusto and amid such approving grins that I fear I often forgot the rascality of the acts in the humour of the narration.

I used to get up every morning as soon as daylight appeared, and descending from the chamber of horrors would betake myself to a seat in the kitchen, when the torments of the night would soon be forgotten in the mazes of " tupto " and " didomi." The old man who kept the dosshouse, named Hughie Devlin, on finding me every morning engrossed in my book, gave me a reputation for sanctity so ill-deserved that it amused me exceedingly. The good man, as well as my fellow-lodgers, with their bookish horizon limited to Bibles and prayer books, honestly believed that it must be one of these I was reading, and treated me with the utmost respect, especially as I seldom exchanged a word with them.

Old Hughie always wore the swallow-tailed coat, knee-breeches and concertina hat which Cockney caricaturists so cleverly and so kindly bestow on all Irishmen. During a residence of over thirty years, extending over the four provinces, I have not seen a dozen men rigged out like that.

It was only five nights in the week that I was doomed to Hughie's chamber of horrors. I walked home every Saturday night when the day's work was over at six p.m., and returned on Monday morning in time to start at six a.m. The walk home was always performed with a light foot and still lighter heart, for the prospect of spending a whole day and two nights at home with my mother made me the happiest of mortals. She generally walked to meet me about a mile outside our town, and no two lovers ever met with greater raptures of delight.

I continued at this work until the approach of winter, when my mother made a proposal that gave me a very agreeable surprise. This was nothing less than that I should stop at home during the winter months, go to school, and improve myself in my classical education. By denying herself of every little luxury and cutting down her necessities to the very lowest limits she had saved as much as would keep us through the winter months. When one remembers that my wages were only five shillings a week, and that this was all she had to live on, with the exception of our garden produce, one may realise what a sacrifice of self that saving must have been.

I, of course, was only too delighted to fall in with the proposal, and so she decided that I should go to the Cookstown Academy, which was, and probably still is, one of the finest schools in Ulster, and a favourite seat of classic learning renowned for the success of its pupils.

At the time I entered it Cookstown Academy was in an exceptionally flourishing condition—filled with the sons of the local gentry, of the professional men and well-to-do business people. Its principal was T. G. Houston, M.A., a distinguished graduate of the Queen's University, who is, I am delighted to say, still alive and well, and enjoying the repose of honours well won. I owe so much to this gentleman that my feelings towards him are more than I can express in mere words ; no one has ever stood or deserved to stand higher in my esteem. If my life had borne no fruits but his friendship I should consider it had not been lived in vain. Before I knew him I thought him rather stiff and stand-offish, and so I approached him with some diffidence. But in the luminous depths of his soft brown eyes I might have seen a soul overflowing with tenderness and humour.

Ah me I how well I remember the Saturday night I was ushered into his presence, and what a formal reception he gave me. On my explaining the object of my visit, he was very naturally surprised that a working cartmaker should wish to study the Latin and Greek classics for the pure love thereof, and suggested that mathematics would be far more useful in my trade; to which, of course, I agreed, but preferred the pleasant to the useful, and would probably have never touched the classics if I had considered them of the slightest practical utility. This attitude of mine hardly prejudiced him in my favour, but at any rate he agreed to take me on my agreeing to his terms of one guinea per quarter for Latin and Greek only.

On the following Monday morning to school I went with a very keen sense of what a ridiculous figure I should cut. For here was I, a workingman, in a second-hand Sunday coat, aged twenty-two, but looking at least ten years older, with my hair turning grey and my shoulders bent, going as a schoolmate amongst a lot of well-dressed boys whose parents, imbued with a sense of their own respectability, would sniff derisively at my pretensions and feel shocked to see their sons recognise me on the street. It was this bitter self-consciousness I had to contend against ; and I did it, too, successfully, for had not my mother taught me to consider myself as good as anybody else; and if some people considered me ridiculous had I not far more reason to consider them contemptible?

If I showed some moral courage in taking this step, I am sure Mr. Houston showed far more in accepting me amongst his pupils, and if any of my townspeople judged me in the way I imagined they never showed it by word or deed in my presence. When I entered school for the first time some of the boys told me afterwards that they thought I was a workman called in to do some repairs. But whatever their thoughts may have been, my good master had the consummate grace to turn them in my favour, for he sent me home before the closing hour, and when I had gone called all the boys to attention, and informed them that I was a particular friend of his, and that they must treat me with marked respect. Now, I verily believe that this was the first time he ever made a pleasing fiction do duty for an ugly fact, and when the Recording Angel made an entry of it in his big book, the Angel of Charity, who corrects all such entries, took good care to erase it with his pencil of light.

My progress at school was somewhat of a disappointment, but it was a disappointment that did me much good, for it helped to cure me of the conceit from which I suffered in no small degree, and from which many self-taught men unfortunately do suffer unconsciously. For the first time in my life I had to recognise that there were young people in the world quite as brilliant as myself, nay, perhaps even more so; in fact, I began to find out that after all I might be a bit of a slow-coach. But in extenuation I found I was unable to turn my opportunities to the best advantage, inasmuch as I was distracted from school work by attending to household duties, for in order to save my mother as much as possible I did the cooking, washing, carrying of water, and so forth. However, at the end of the quarter the master complimented me on the progress I had made as he handed me his account. I then found that instead of the stipulated fee of one guinea, he had put down ten shillings, and when I laid this on the desk before him he pushed it back towards me. I did not pick it up, but was so overcome with his generosity that I was unable to speak and hurried out with tears in my eyes.

When I went to school next morning he called me into his senior English class and told the pupils he was very pleased to see me amongst them. From my extensive reading I was well up in English, especially literature, but at the same time my hand-writing was so execrably bad that I was put to write pot-hooks, so that I was in the unique position of touching two extremes. I thus continued for about another term, making respectable progress not only in Latin and Greek, but in other branches of learning, when, to my great sorrow, our good master was promoted as principal of the Coleraine Academical Institute. I was so choked with grief on our fare-well handshaking that I was unable to thank him for all he had done for me, and he told me that if he had continued in our town he would have made me an assistant. He would accept no remuneration, but asked me to promise that I should do as much for any of my fellow-creatures in the same position as myself as he had done for me ; happily I was after-wards able to fulfil this condition.

I never met a more perfect type of the scholar and

the gentleman, and I would add of the Christian, if Christians only practised what they professed. He was so scrupulously upright that he would not allow his pupils to purchase books at the National Schools where they were sold at one-half their value for the benefit of the poorer classes and at the expense of the taxpayer. His pupils, being the children of well-to-do parents, must not act meanly by taking advantage of a privilege not meant for them.

He was so broad in his religious views that he would not teach English History to his Catholic pupils because he could find no text book that he could conscientiously put into their hands.

All his pupils loved him as much as they respected him—a combination of feeling on the part of pupils which few teachers are able to evoke ; for my own part, much as I learned from his teaching I learned still more from his example.

Mr. Houston was succeeded by his assistant, a very amiable and good-natured soul, but rather lacking in the strength of character that distinguished his predecessor ; and though he was almost equally able to win the affections of his pupils he was less able to win their respect. He had been Chairman of the Debating Society in which I had previously figured, so that he knew me very well, and from knowing had become my friend. At the recommendation of Mr. Houston he took me as his pupil and kindly allowed the question of fees to stand over until such time as I should be able to settle without difficulty, a period which arrived a few years afterwards, to our mutual satisfaction.

I was with him a short time only when he gave me a piece of advice that became the great turning-point in my life and opened up a dazzling vista of possibilities. It was to the effect that I should study for a literary scholarship in the Queen's College, Galway, where he himself had been a student of some distinction. He recommended Galway as being better for my purpose than Cork or Belfast, the other constituent colleges of the Queen's University. In Galway the competition was not so keen, and therefore my chance of a scholarship was so much the better ; again, living and lodging were cheaper, the place was quieter and the surroundings more salubrious and beautiful. The proposal filled me with delight, and raised my ambition to a height it had never soared before, and so I eagerly acceded to it. I then consulted my mother, that oracle whose judgment always proved unerring, and she was almost as much elated as myself at the prospect thus opened up. When I pointed out the difficulties in which my absence would place her and the anguish of our separating, she pooh-poohed it. As her life was drawing to a close, she argued, why should the prospects of the life that was opening before me be spoiled for the sake of her short existence ? In fact, it would make that short existence still shorter if she realised that it stood in the way of my welldoing ; but on the other hand it would be prolonged and brightened if she realised I was doing well, even though far apart from her.

Although this reasoning convinced me, it aroused some qualms of conscience which after the lapse of some forty-five years are not yet wholly eased.

Having obtained a prospectus from the College I at once set about preparing for the examination, with seven or eight months to complete the task. The ground I had to break up was for the most part new, for with the exception of Virgil and Sallust

the other writers were quite strangers to me.   In
Latin they included the Satires and Epistles of Horace,
two books of Livy, and Cicero on the Manilian Law,
together with Composition, History, and Geography.
In Greek there was Xenophon's *Anabasis* ; two books
of the *Iliad*, and the *Phœnissae* of Euripides, with
Composition, History, and Geography thrown in.
This work did not appear to me half so formidable
as   the   Matriculation   course,   which   comprised
Mathematics, which, with the exception of a little
arithmetic, was to me as much of a mystery as the
science and art of wigmaking.   I not only knew
nothing about Algebra and Euclid, but when I commenced to learn them positively loathed them, and
found that I was not only slow in learning them,
but downright stupid, forgetting with ease what I
had learned with difficulty.   And yet I had to pass
an examination in them at the end of a few months !
My literary studies were my pleasure, but this was
my toil—the dragon that guarded the golden fruit
which I had determined to pluck.

Some time previous to this telegraph works had
been started by the Government close to our house.
As the wages were good I was persuaded to apply
for a job.   I did so, and sure enough got it.   At this
work I could earn not five shillings a week, but five
shillings a day, but, at the same time, if I yielded to
the temptation of earning big wages I must sacrifice
the prospect of going to College.   I compromised on
the matter with the concurrence of my employer ;
I worked two days in the week, Friday and Saturday,
and on the other four days went to school and worked
for the scholarship.   On the two days that I worked
I was not only able to earn as much as kept us
through the week, but even a surplus to put aside
for my entrance fee to the College.

There were some fifteen men besides myself engaged in the work, and with one or two exceptions I found them all very kindly disposed towards me. They were all oath-bound Orangemen, and nearly all illiterates, for whom I used to sign the receipts for their weekly wages, and I found ample reason to attribute their sectarianism to ignorance and not to any natural perversity.

With regard to my attendance at the Academy, the master had a pupil whom he was coaching for a scholarship in Belfast, and up to a certain point his course of study and mine were identical, and the master coached us together. But when our courses diverged the master found he had no time to coach us separately, so I was compelled to plough the rest of my furrow alone. He was good enough to give me a piece of advice to the effect that I should translate that portion of the Greek play set in the examination not literally but into verse ! for D'Arcy Thompson, the professor, was himself a poet, and would thus give me double marks. If I had followed this advice I might have got double marks, but it would have been for the amusement I had caused D'Arcy, who was a humorist of the first order. I managed somehow to get to the end of it all right, except in the mathematical portion, where I felt wobbly.

As the time for my departure drew near I was confronted with the problem of ways and means, but found that my good genius had already faced that problem and partly solved it. She had saved about five pounds out of my earnings, and placed it at my disposal, reserving nothing for her own support while saying she had plenty. I could not think of leaving her thus, but even if I had taken this sum it would have been hardly sufficient.

I should be obliged to pay for five courses : Latin, Greek, Modern Languages, Mathematics, and English Literature, each course being £2 ; but only the half of this had to be paid on entrance and the other half at the commencement of the second term, and in the case of a scholar not at all. There was besides 10s. for matriculation fee, so that the sum total of my fees would amount to £5 10s. Then there was my railway fare, 16s., and the same for my return in case I failed, and 10s. for my keep during the examination week ; so that altogether I should require £7 12s.

In making up this sum I found that I had more friends than I ever knew, and they, having seen or heard of my difficulty, came to the rescue without being asked by me, and made up the deficit and even more. In fact, I could have obtained the whole amount if I had chosen to ask for it. One friend offered to advance it without any security beyond my promise to pay it at my convenience. However, I accepted nothing beyond the necessary £7 10s., and the most of that was from my mother's savings. My teacher presented me with his college gown, and my former teacher, Mr. Houston, sent me a black frock-coat of superfine broadcloth, which was much too large for me. This worn in combination with an old billycock hat, a collarless shirt, not entirely concealed by a red cravat, and nondescript waistcoat and trousers, must have given me as bizarre an appearance as ever figured on a variety stage.

The night before my departure was the saddest in my life, and the memory of it haunts me still—a lifelong sore never to be uncovered without tears. We sat up all through the night exchanging counsels of solace and encouragement. Why, she reasoned, should I be downhearted? I had only to feel confident of success, and I should be sure to win it. Even if I did not succeed, I would be all the better for making the effort, and must try again with renewed hope. I had nothing to lose, for as long as I had my health and my hands to work with I should be no worse off than when I started. I must not worry about her, for she would be happy in thinking of my success, of which she felt quite sure. In this way she sought to cheer me up, and at the same time conceal her own feelings, which she never allowed to overcome her, at least in my presence. But now and again she would go outside to get, as she said, a mouthful of fresh air, and I could hear her sobs, each of which stabbed me to the heart; then she would come in and resume her talk with a smiling face.

I had to start early, and at daybreak had breakfast, which I hardly touched, and the bottle of stout which she had brought in unknown, as a final treat, I was quite unable to drink. Some of my workmates were going on a jaunting-car as far as Dungannon, and as my railway journey to Galway began there they promised to give me a lift so far. I had an old wooden box into which I put a second shirt and a few text books, and putting a copy of Euclid in my pocket, was ready to start when the car arrived. Having shaken hands with the kindly neighbours who had called to bid me good-bye and wish me luck, and taken a sad farewell of my mother, off I started. Throughout this nine miles drive to Dungannon I was too full to exchange a word with my workmates, and at the same time the tear never left my eye. They noticed it, and did not bother me with talk.

As soon as I got into the train for Galway I pulled out my Euclid in the hope of refreshing my memory on its contents. It was a vain hope. I could not assimilate the least portion of that mess, and only bewildered my poor brain in trying to do so, and yet I persisted in trying even till the end of the journey.

I arrived in the good old City of the Tribes about nine p.m., and a wet dark night it was, seeming as it were to sympathise with my own feelings. Shouldering my box, I walked from the station to the central square, and asked a policeman to show me to a decent lodging-house. He did so, and much to my surprise I found it not only decent, but clean and comfortable, quite unlike my experience in Magherafelt. The tariff, to be sure, was much higher, being sixpence per night instead of twopence, but the value was well worth the difference.

Although I did not sleep the previous night I slept very little during that night thinking on the ordeal that awaited me on the morrow. When the morrow arrived I strolled over to the College with my gown carefully bundled under my arm, and the fees still more carefully stowed away in my trousers pocket. If anything could have put me in good spirits it would have been the sight of that building, the most beautiful I had ever seen, with the grounds around it equally beautiful. It is a reduced replica of Christchurch College, Oxford, and the finest building in the province of Connacht. But on that particular morning its beauty seemed to mock me, and repelled rather than invited.

I loitered around the grounds, watching the professors enter, and speculating which of them was to be my tormentor. At last I saw one person enter with a pinched and puckered face overcast with a very hard expression, rendered still harder by a monocle screwed into his right orbit, and I shuddered and said, " That figure must be my tormentor, the Professor of Mathematics." I was quite right in my diagnosis, and during my subsequent attendance on his lectures he fully realised my first impressions. But afterwards when I was no longer his pupil I found him a very amiable gentleman, and so kindly disposed towards me that he appointed me Latin tutor to his son and daughter.

To make a long story short, I paid my fees and got registered, but when the Registrar heard my name, he asked me, Did I spell it with an *i* or an *e*, and in my usual absent-minded manner I promptly said " Yes," and he equally absentmindedly put it down with an *i* ; and so it has remained ever since, though up till then I had always put it down with an *a*.

I had, of course, no difficulty in passing the literary portion of the Matriculation, but when it came to the hard-faced Professor with his infernal mathematics, I said to myself : " Now, Jimmy, you're in for it " ; but, marvellous to relate, I floundered through the Arithmetic and Algebra far easier than I expected ; but when it came to Euclid—O, what a mess I got into ! The enemy plied me with problem after problem, and I found each of them a blind alley that led nowhere. At last he asked me to bisect a given finite straight line, which seemed too good to be serious. I looked at his face—but no, there was no gleam of humour in it, indeed, it was the last face in the world where one would expect to see such a phenomenon, he was solemnly serious, so I tackled his straight line and cut it in two, Heaven

II

only knows how. Even when I had done so he was not satisfied, for he told me I should not use the word " cut," but " bisected," so I at once used this blessed word, which seemed to relieve him very much, and he let me off without more ado.

When I got outside the torture chamber I heaved a deep sigh of relief, like a criminal just reprieved from the clutches of the executioner.

Having thus passed the lion in my path, I had no difficulty with the scholarship examination which came on the day after ; and when its results were announced I had the supreme satisfaction of seeing my name third on the list of five.

I then fondly imagined that all before me was smooth water and easy sailing. Alas ! I little dreamt that I had only emerged from one sea of trouble to embark on another.

CHAPTER VI

It was no wonder if the struggle of preparing for this examination, and the anxiety of going through it, were a terrible strain on my nervous system, which was morbidly sensitive even from birth. When I remember how I felt that strain, the wonder is that I stood it so well. I struggled hard to conceal it from all the outside world, but, in spite of that, the professors who examined my papers diagnosed it in the tremulous character of my handwriting. In fact they diagnosed it to such an extent that Doctor, afterwards Sir W. T. Moffett, then Registrar, and also Professor of English Literature, Metaphysics, and History, one of the most amiable souls imaginable, approached me on the subject and told me that he and his colleagues had observed with regret my state of health, as shown in the papers I had sent in. They considered I should have absolute rest and medical advice in order to avoid a breakdown, which the severe course of studies, imposed on me as a scholar, was likely to entail.

As I had not the means and still less the inclination to let this well-meant damper fall on my hopes, I thanked him for it, but told him I would persist in the course and attend the prescribed lectures at all hazards. My first care was to secure suitable diggings, and in this I was materially assisted by making the acquaintance of a fellow-student named O'Brien, from Clare. Like myself he had just entered, but unlike myself he was a medical. He had such a sober, steady and God-fearing appearance, and his clothes were such a protest against everything suggestive of the fashionable and the frivolous that my heart warmed to him. He informed me that he was lodging with the family of a police sergeant, and that they might take me in as his fellow-lodger. Accordingly I went there and was shown into a sitting and bedroom on the top floor, and told I might share the same with Mr. O'Brien for three shillings per week, the sum to include cooking. I closed on the offer, and having conveyed my old box and its contents to this domicile installed myself therein and opened a new chapter in the history of my life.

The question of food supply, as it may be called in these war times, was the problem I had next to study. It was very simple ; I wanted only as much as would keep body and soul together, and for this I calculated about sixpence per day would suffice. I purveyed my food and the landlady cooked it as per agreement. I used to purchase cocoa nibs by the pound, and a portion of these prepared in boiling water made an infusion which, taken without sugar or milk, but with dry bread only, constituted my breakfast and supper, and cost about fourpence. My dinner consisted of a few potatoes and a fried herring, which cost about twopence—the whole day's bill of fare amounting thus to the sum I had calculated on. During the first college term from the end of October till the beginning of the Christmas vacation this was my daily *régime*, never once broken by the taste of milk, sugar, or butcher's meat, and never exceeding sixpence daily—a rate that would make ordinary economy seem the height of extravagance. When the few shillings I possessed were expended, my mother, to whom I wrote weekly, by pinching herself even worse, I suppose, than I was pinched, managed to send me as much as tided me over the remainder of the term.

After all, in spite of every drawback, I should have been comparatively happy but for my unfortunate backwardness in the Mathematical course. Being a scholar, I was obliged to attend the lectures three times a week, and every lecture was an hour of agony. The lectures implied preparation, and at the very least two-thirds of my time were spent at this drudgery to the hindrance of my Greek, Latin, and German preparation. At almost every blessed lecture the professor would single me out, from a class of about a hundred and fifty pupils, to work problems on the blackboard. Even if I had been an expert, I could not have done it in the presence of so many strange faces all levelled at me. But being by no means an expert, and at the same time afflicted with morbid sensibility and a tremulous hand, I fairly broke down on one occasion and withdrew to my seat. He kept me in after the lecture and gave me a very severe reprimand—going to the length of saying that I was giving a very bad example to his class and making a show of myself.

In acting towards me in this manner I was bound to admit that he was only doing what he considered his duty, and doing it too for my future benefit. But at the same time I could not help feeling that he did it in a way that gave me intense pain without tending to help me on. Nay, then, it did help indirectly, for it enabled me to realise that I was not a born genius, and if I wanted to succeed in the new career I had chosen it must be by hard work, and hard work only.

As I look back at the first term of my first session it seems the very saddest period of an existence checkered with many such. I felt low-spirited, heart-sick, and out of humour with myself and all the rest of the world. I took no exercise except a solitary walk in the afternoon along the seaside or around the docks, when I almost envied the sailors going out to sea, and never looked in the direction of my home in the north without moist eyes. But this moisture passed away, or rather became the moisture of joy, when the Christmas vacation came on and I started for the home I had been pining for. My joy was heightened with the reflection that if I arrived in Galway with a heavy heart and a light purse I was now leaving it with a light heart and a heavy purse, for I was carrying home £12 10s., the first instalment of my scholarship; and to me, who had never touched such a sum before, it seemed a princely fortune, still further enhanced by the way in which it was won.

When I got home the reception I received more than repaid me for all the privation and anxiety I had gone through. My mother, however, told me I had done nothing more than she expected, but even if I had failed and returned without a penny in my pocket my welcome from her would have been no different; possibly it might have been warmer, for pity would then be mingled with affection. I received many congratulations from well-to-do people who had never recognised me before, and also many from people of my own class, especially those who jeered bitterly against me when I started, and who would have done so again had I come back a failure. However, I could now afford to be magnanimous, so I took all in good part.

I was asked to call on the leading tailor of the town, and on doing so was fairly astounded to learn that he had been ordered to measure me for a suit of clothes and had received cloth for that purpose. It was accompanied with a very gracious message to the effect that I must not consider it a charitable donation, but a well-won tribute to my industry. I was never able to ascertain who the giver or givers were, but I suspected some of the friends whom I had formerly found while connected with the Cookstown Library or Debating Society.

The incident reminded me very forcibly of the story of Dr. Johnson and the shoes left at his door, and so indignantly kicked away, and I debated within myself whether I should act in the same manner. My decision was to do nothing of the sort ; the gift was not intended as an insult, but as a benefit badly wanted and offered in a friendly spirit, and to reject it would seem very like smacking a friend in the face. Besides all this, the affectation of wounded pride would only make me appear ridiculous. So I accepted the gift, and for the first time in my life got measured for a new suit.

My employment as carpenter in the telegraph works was still open for me, so I went back and resumed it as if I had only left the day before yesterday, and continued at it all through the vacation, earning about thirty shillings a week. My old workmates gave me a right royal reception, and not content with congratulating me individually they formed a procession and chaired me through the works ; and I on my part, as in duty bound, acknowledged the honour by standing drinks all round.

When I started for College at the end of the vacation it was under auspices quite different from those of my first start ; there was no heart heaviness nor moisture of the eyes on my part and no sobbings on the part of my mother. We were both in excellent spirits, and looked on the future not only with hope, but with absolute confidence. The lectures of the second term opened in my favour ; for those on Euclid were at an end, and those on Arithmetic and Algebra had taken their place, and although I was, Heaven knows, backward enough on these two subjects, I was not so adverbially stupid on them as on the other one.

The lectures on English Literature had also commenced, and herein I got my innings. My lifelong and multifarious reading stood to me in good stead, and proved that after all I was not such a duffer as some of my fellow-students might have imagined. Far as I stood below them in the mathematical course I stood equally far above them in this, and I fancied I saw a decided change in their demeanour towards me. The professor, Dr. T. W. Moffett, complimented me on the extent of my reading, and became a friend of mine to such a degree that one day he thrust a five-pound note into my hand, remarking that I might find it useful and I could repay him any time I found it convenient. Some considerable time afterwards I did so, and he seemed, or affected to seem, quite surprised, saying that he never expected repayment. During all the remainder of my stay at the College I was invariably invited to all his dinner parties.

With the Greek, Latin and German professors I was on equally good terms, and would find it difficult to say which of them I liked the most. I think, however, that the Professor of Greek, D'Arcy Thompson, stood highest in my admiration—no man whom I ever met coming nearer my conception of the Great Man. Amongst the other professors he figured like the Olympian Jove in an assembly of the Dii Majores. He had a magnificent presence crowned with the domed forehead which ancient Art always placed on the " Father of the Gods." He overflowed with humour, which revealed itself in the everlasting twinkle of his large, blue eyes. His voice was in harmony with his other gifts, sounding like the deep-toned music of a grand organ, and to hear him recite Homer in the original was like listening to the roll of the sea. No wonder he was a universal favourite and in such request at all the dinner parties and social gatherings in Galway ; and when he began to pour forth his tide of humour in that rich voice nobody else would venture to speak except in roars of laughter. His books are masterpieces of English literature, and I am glad to see that one of them, *Day Dreams of a Schoolmaster*, has been lately republished.

To have secured the friendship of such a man was something to be proud of, and that was my privilege.

The Professor of Latin, if not so gifted either in mind or body, was no less an extraordinary personality, and like his colleague was a humorist, as is shown in his pamphlets and his contributions to *Kottabos*, the magazine of his Alma Mater, Dublin University. He was also a profound metaphysician and the author of a work on the " Platonic Idea." Known as Dr. Thomas Maguire, we always called him Tommy. He became notorious in after years as the payer of £700 to Pigott for the forged letter that led to the " Parnell Inquiry," to which he was summoned as a witness, and died rather suddenly before giving evidence. He was a staunch friend and a bitter enemy, and would go through fire and water to a friend's assistance or an enemy's ruin. Amongst those whom he hated most were the leaders of his own faith and nationality, owing to their support of sectarian education, which was the *bête noire* of his existence. Their press invariably spoke of him in the most scurrilous terms, and he paid them back with compound interest. His appearance was by no means dignified, for he was short and squattish, and walked with a splay-footed waddle. He became not only my friend but my familiar, and, in spite of some of his views, which were the antithesis of my own, I held him in the highest esteem, for I judged him, as I judge everybody else, by the qualities of the heart rather than by those of the head.

The professor of modern languages was a German named Geisler, a Doctor of Philosophy of Heidelberg University. He, too, was an extraordinary character, and became a great friend of mine. He always opened his lectures by cracking jokes with me, and said he could never look into my face without reciprocating my smile. In reading Schiller's *Gedichte*, he always called on me to do it in English, remarking that I must be a poet from the spirit I put into the translation. If he had seen some of the verses I had been guilty of making I am sure he might not have called me a poet. He also said I had quite a talent for learning languages, and strongly advised me to go as a teacher of English to Russia. He himself had been a teacher in Petersburg, and promised me some introductions if I went there.

Such were my friends amongst the professors— they are all, alas ! dead and gone, but their memories still live shrined in the gratitude of at least one old student.

When I began to feel my way amongst the students, the more I knew of them the better I liked them. They were on the whole a body of young men of unaffected manners, healthy morals, and quite untainted with priggishness or snobbery, but willing to honour merit even in the poorest amongst them. In fact, the only qualities to which they rendered homage were scholastic attainments and athletic prowess. The majority of them, in fact the overwhelming majority, had come to Galway for the same reasons as myself—good education and economic living. They were far removed from the extravagant and reckless type of student that one reads about in novels, and they never allowed the animal spirits with which they overflowed to carry them into mischievous excesses, so that they stood fairly high in the good graces of the general community, even though viewed askance by the priests.

They were divided into two well-defined types, Northerners and Southerners, between whom lay a world of difference, though both belonging to the same middle classes. The Northerners were quiet, plodding, and persevering, possessing all the qualities that command respect rather than admiration, and though by no means brilliant were nearly always successful. The Southerners, on the other hand, were more successful in brilliant dash than steady persistence, more prodigal than parsimonious, more addicted to sport and less to study, more capable of winning friendship than respect. They had more failures than the Northerners ; but at the same time more brilliant exceptionals. By Northerners were meant only those who, like myself, came from Ulster. While each set kept pretty well to itself I was usually at home with both, attracted to the one by similarity

of associations and ideals, and to the other by con-
geniality of temperament. I found many friends on
both sides, and my outlook was beginning to brighten
when the end of the session darkened it worse than
ever.

The Professor of Mathematics had already
threatened to reject me at the sessional examination ;
and sure enough he was as good as his word, for he
plucked me to the very last feather. This was a
knock-down blow and no mistake, for it meant that
I was to forfeit £12 10s., the remaining half of my
scholarship, as well as three prizes in Latin, German,
and English Literature. But it also meant that I
was to go home as penniless as when I first left it
and resume my work as a carpenter—a miserable
failure in the eyes of all who knew me, and worse
perhaps than anything else, appearing the same in
my own eyes. I did not flatter my wounded vanity
with the pleasing illusion that finds favour with so
many students in a similar position, to the effect
that they failed through no fault of their own but
through the unfairness of the examiner. No ; I
faced the hard fact, and, like Dr. Johnson, admitting
a mistake of his to a lady, put it down to " Ignorance,
gross Ignorance," and told any friend who took the
trouble to ask me that the examiner only did his
duty, but would have exceeded it if he had given me a
single mark.

When I got home, I had to face three tasks. The
first and foremost was to work for the support of
my mother and myself ; the second was to work
for the supplemental examination which would allow
me the chance of winning back the forfeited half
of my scholarship ; and the third was to work for
the new scholarship of the second and third years.

Fortunately, I had invincible confidence in myself, and never for a moment doubted my capacity for getting through the task before me. So back I went to work at the telegraph poles amongst my old mates, and at this I continued all through the summer months. The greater part of my spare time was spent at the mathematical drudgery, wherein I got on much better than at college, for I was able to think more clearly when outside the fog of the lecture-room. My studies for the second and third years' scholarships were only pleasant interludes, which included German and English in addition to the Ancient Classics, and were easily got through.

When the examination approached in the latter end of October I went off to meet it with a confidence of success which the result justified. I emerged from the torture-chamber with flying colours, and next day had the supreme satisfaction of pocketing the £12 10s which had been held back pending my ordeal. But according to a rule of the College I was to forfeit the sessional prizes. However, in spite of this rule I decided on making an effort to secure them, and so I sent a strongly-worded letter to the Council drawing their attention to the fact that it was hardly equitable that I, who had only left the workshop for the College, should be placed on the same footing as students who had been properly trained for the Matriculation; that I was not only handicapped by the fact that I had never been taught Mathematics, but handicapped still more by the feeble state of my health, which prevented my applying myself to study with the concentration necessary for success. The Council admitted the force of my contention, and agreeing that mine was an exceptional case, decided to break the rule in my favour and let me have the prizes.

I now stood on equal terms with my fellow-students who had so far outdistanced me at the end of the session ; in fact, I was vain enough to imagine that I had outdistanced them, for their work of preparation for the second and third years scholarships seemed a rather puny piece of business compared with the struggle I had gone through. That struggle made me feel equal to any difficulties that might rise before me in the future, and confirmed me in the self-confidence I had always felt. This personal experience, and subsequent observations, have enabled me to feel sure that no man can succeed unless he feels quite sure that he is able to do so. Loss of self-confidence means loss of success.

Conscious of this fact, I competed for the second and third years scholarship and retained my old place of third on the list.

I was now done with the lectures on pure mathematics, but had to attend the course in mathematical physics, and that was like falling from the frying-pan into the fire ; and to descend from the lectures on English Literature into those of Logic, which were now obligatory, was a descent from noon-day into twilight. However, I got through the session without a hitch, but at the next examination for the half B.A. degree, I once more met the usual lion on my path. On this occasion the lion was not one professor but six, being two from each of the three colleges, who took me in hand consecutively and left me like a fowl prepared for the pot. This knock-down was far worse than the preceding, for it imperilled two scholarships and also the B.A. degree ; and worse still, would tend to lower me in the eyes of my fellow-students. Although I had done well in the literary subjects I would get no credit for them, but would have to go over the entire course again. It was as gloomy a prospect as I ever faced, and my intense susceptibility deepened the gloom. However, I fortified myself with the reflection that if it came to the worst I could be no worse than when I started, as long as I was able to use my hands ; and at once decided on doing what I had done before—making a renewed effort and putting double energy into it.

This examination was held in October, and I went back to College to attend lectures for my third and last session, which commenced in November. The supplemental examination which I felt bound to go through was to take place in January, so that I had about two months to work for it.

When I got back the first mathematical scholar in the College, by name O'Kinealy, an exceedingly brilliant man who afterwards became a leading advocate at the Calcutta bar, volunteered to coach me through the entire course I had failed in. But my confidence, conceit, or whatever it might be called, would not allow me to accept the friendly offer, so I thanked him for it, saying that I was so ashamed of myself that I was determined to sink or swim by my own effort and without help. I do not think that he esteemed me the less for my resolve, and his friendship is still dearly treasured in my memory, while he himself has gone over to the majority.

I worked so hard at these subjects that I actually turned my loathing of them into a liking, and if I were starting my studies anew I should put them on the same footing, and cultivate them with the same ardour as I would cultivate literary subjects. At first I looked upon these mathematical subjects, for which I had no inclination and little capacity, as being completely useless in my case ; but I afterwards found that in wrestling with them my mental powers acquired an adaptability for tackling any branch of knowledge I might require, just as the pounding of a sack of sawdust is useful to a boxer when he tackles an opponent in the ring.

Although I worked so hard for this examination I was in a state of nervous fear about the result, for it was not unlikely my whole future would turn upon it. So in order to improve my chances I took two modern languages, French and German, instead of one, thereby increasing the sum total of my marks. In the interval between the end of the examination and the declaration of results I strolled through the streets of Dublin on the look-out for a workshop where I might be likely to drop on employment in case I again came a cropper, which would have rendered my return to College impossible—at least for some indefinite time. Happily, such a contingency did not arise, for somehow I managed to satisfy the examiners, and, though the success may perhaps have been won by the skin of my teeth only, it was a very big matter for me, and meant that all my troubles for the B.A. degree were now at an end. My work for the final examination would be no longer a work but a labour of love.

I went back to College to prepare for this examination, and the subjects I selected were English Literature, History, and Metaphysics—a course that was both delightful and instructive, and second to none in widening the intellectual outlook and in cultivating a sympathy with all that is best in human nature. At the end of the session I returned home, and to my trade as usual, and in October sat for the Degree Examination.

The fortune of war had now turned, and I passed with second class honours, which were the highest given in those subjects at that examination.

All the joy I might have felt on this occasion when I returned home was changed to grief, the most abiding grief of my life, for I found my mother dying. She, however, lived long enough to recognise me and to feel that I had not disappointed her hopes, and that feeling soothed her last moments.

I am sure I loved her as much as any human being ever loved a mother, and no mother ever lived more worthy of such love. But beyond that, I revered her as an oracle whose forecasts had never erred, and a mentor whose advice had always filled me with hope and courage. During her long life she never incurred a debt even to the extent of a shilling, and never spent a penny on any superfluities in the way of food or drink ; and when the men, women, and children of Ireland were flocking in crowds to receive the pledge from the hands of Father Mathew, the great Apostle of Temperance, my father would never allow her to take it, insisting that in her case it would only be a needless humiliation.

She was a wonderful judge of character, and her prescience, deduced from keen observation, amounted to a power that seemed prophetic. Of this she was so conscious that she often said she never liked to predict evil, lest her forecast should prove true. Here is one very remarkable example of her power. A certain young man in those days was my best and dearest friend. We were inseparable companions and loved each other better perhaps than brothers. From his frequent visits to our house my mother had an opportunity of studying him at close quarters, and the result was that she cautioned me to beware

I

of him, for he would rob me at the first opportunity, and, strange to say, he did so. It happened some time after her death that I was leaving Cookstown for Galway, and he asked me to sleep with him that night. I thought of my mother's words, but resented the suspicion to which they gave rise, as being mean and unworthy of myself and unjust to him. So I accepted the invitation, and during the night when I was fast asleep my pocket was picked.

I had borrowed five pounds the previous day to start me for the College session and carefully tied it in a knot in my pocket handkerchief. When I got to Portadown I pulled out the handkerchief to get my train fare and the knot was still on it, but the note was gone. I had not a penny left, and might have stopped there, but, fortunately, the Catholic curate of Cookstown was travelling by the same train, and to him I told the story. He very kindly lent me a pound, which saved the situation and enabled me to proceed to Galway. My friend, the pickpocket, knowing that I would "blow" upon him, set about vilifying me in the most villainous manner amongst our friends, so that any subsequent talk of mine might be discounted. He was one of the most cunning men I ever knew, and had told me years before that he had been in the habit of picking his brother's pocket in the night, and that he always covered the theft by cutting a hole in the pocket.

Of course, he and I became deadly enemies, but in spite of that, and without my knowledge, he painted a little cross which I had placed as a temporary mark over my mother's grave. Now, why should he do so? Well, before going to America he had evidently gone to confession, and was told that he must make reparation for his theft, and I well knew this was how he did it.

Intending to return to Ireland a few years afterwards, he embarked with all his belongings on board a ship at New York, but finding that the ship would not leave for several hours he went ashore, and was never seen afterwards alive or dead.

CHAPTER VII

A new chapter in my life commenced with my permanent removal from Cookstown, my native place, to dear old Galway, the city of my choice; and with the permanent giving up of my trade and my transition from the workman into the student. This transition was very easily effected, for my heart never warmed to the trade, and beyond the indispensable two-foot rule, I never purchased a tool pertaining to it. And yet it is wonderful how its habits stuck to me long afterwards; for when a baker friend of mine in Galway showed me his new bread cart I had no sooner cast my eyes over the wheels than he said: " Why, you seem to know more about wheels than anybody else." I smiled and said nothing. On another occasion, at a still longer interval, when, as a medical man, I was sawing a board to make a splint for a broken leg, I quite automatically groped for my rule on the left side of my trousers; and the mother of the patient when she observed me use the saw remarked that I handled it like a skilled workman.

When I returned to the College as a graduate I was eligible to compete for a senior scholarship of the value of £40; seven of these being attached to the College. So I prepared for the one in Modern Languages and Literature, selecting French, German, and English. Although the course was a very long one, I managed to pull through it and secured the £40.

I was now comparatively well off, but instead of resting on my oars I embarked on the courses of anatomy, chemistry, botany, and zoology, with a view of proceeding to the degree in Medicine. About the same time, too, I commenced to work as a " Coach " in preparing students for the Matriculation examination. At this work I will take the liberty of saying I was very successful, and soon had my hands full of it, thereby earning from £2 to £3 weekly. I not only coached my pupils in the classical part of this examination, but had even the audacity to coach them in the mathematical part—the part in which I myself had proved such a flagrant failure. In fact, I brought them quite successfully over the ground on which I had so often stumbled ; and I never until then knew that the best way to learn a subject is to commence teaching it.

The new domains of knowledge on which I had now entered, so boundless in their extent and so magnificent in their produce, compelled me to lower my estimate of the fields I had passed through in reaching the B.A. degree. I realised that the man whose learning is limited to books alone is like the man whose knowledge of Nature is limited to the study of pictures, and his judgment on the great questions affecting the life of the world is always or often based on insufficient data, and his opinions rendered lop-sided and extravagant.

Of this we have had a flagrant example in the frenzied professors of Germany.

At the end of the first year's medical course I allowed myself to be turned aside from it by a suggestion of my friend, Dr. Moffett. He approached me and promised to get me a nomination for an Inspectorship of Schools, at a salary, if I remember rightly, of £300 per annum. He furthermore informed me that if I proceeded to the degree of Doctor in Laws it would be a tremendous advantage. As this afforded me the prospect of conquering a new world I assented, and dropping the other courses I commenced the course for this. But I never took kindly to it, and much of the year was lost in taking things too easy and relaxing the bow which had been so long and so rigidly bent.

It was not, however, all lost time, for it brought me into contact with Mills' *Political Economy* and Maine's *Ancient Law*—two works which in themselves are almost a liberal education. I also dawdled over some other works on Political and Economic Science, and on the strength thereof I tried my luck for a Senior Scholarship in Queen's College, Cork, as a variant on Galway. I did not obtain that scholarship, nor indeed did I deserve to, but I obtained a Senior Exhibition of about half the value.

I now began to feel some misgivings about my prospects for a School Inspectorship, and the more I reflected on these prospects the more uncertain they seemed. A nomination in itself would not secure me a place, but would only entitle me to compete for one, in which case my chance of success would be by no means certain—nay, the odds would be very much against me in the mathematical section. If I failed the first time I might be too old before another chance offered, and thus my time might be wasted in working for what was only a chance within a chance. If, on the other hand, I pushed on through the Medical course, at the end of four years, one of which had expired, I felt confident of having an honourable and lucrative profession that would render me independent in any part of the world, which a School Inspectorship would not do.

Accordingly I decided on entering this course again and pushing through it, come in my way what might. On my telling this decision to a friend he remarked, with a toss of his head, that he could never imagine how I should succeed. This remark, to which I made no reply, may not have been intended to hurt me, but it did so to such an extent that I always remembered it as a stimulus to persevere.

Having thus entered on the Medical course I pursued it with far better spirits than I pursued the Arts course. My privations were now at an end, and in the matter of food and clothing I was as well provided as any other student at the College. Instead of the bare necessaries of life I now enjoyed its comforts, which to me were nothing less than luxuries ; and of such luxuries as the place afforded I had my share. I also removed into better " diggings," where I sometimes entertained my friends to the " feasts of Reason and the flow of Soul "—supplemented with other cheer more material and perhaps more exhilarating.

Of my numerous friends, some have passed over to the Great Majority after leaving distinguished records behind them ; others are happily still in the land of the living, which is rendered all the better for their presence therein. No matter in what British possessions they have found homes, their influence is felt in ministering to the social and mental needs of the people—healing their physical ailments, and in fact co-operating in every useful work that adds to the aggregate of human welfare and the greatness and glory of the Empire.

To one of these old friends, whose life service has been devoted to India, I owe a friendship that has existed for some forty years and grows stronger and brighter as it grows older. If I had brought nothing from Galway College but that gift, my career there would not have been passed in vain.

It must not be imagined that all my friends were to be found amongst the students who succeeded. I had, perhaps, still more amongst those who failed, for I never have, and I hope never shall, make success the measure of my friendship ; and if there was one corner of my heart warmer than another it was reserved for the unfortunate " chronics," as our habitual failures were called. Many of these by their good-nature, geniality, and sporting qualities more than counterbalanced their idleness or incapacity for study ; and, after all, the capacity for passing examinations benefits the possessor only, but good nature and geniality give pleasure to everybody with whom they come in contact.

One such case in particular occurs to me. Like myself, he was the son of a widowed mother, but the similarity ends here, for his father was a clergyman. Twice a year for twelve years he went regularly up for the half-degree examination, and as regularly came back plucked. Yet, like many other " chronics," he was by no means stupid, but had good literary gifts and a positive talent for music, and as a dog-fancier his judgment was second to none. His defeats had not soured his disposition, he had a good word for all his associates—even for the examiners, and was hearty in his congratulations to all friends who outstripped him in the race. And yet he was not an idler, for his poor mother told me that she often shed tears watching him sit over his books from dawn till dark.

He and I went together for the *viva voce* examination in anatomy, and when we came out he told me that the only portion of the body he could recognise was the " *tendo Achillis*." The pleasure that I felt on passing was considerably damped by my friend's misfortune. In the end, however, he succeeded in getting the double qual. of Edinburgh (physician's and surgeon's diploma), and I had the pleasure of congratulating him on his being appointed a ship's surgeon. Unfortunately, he did not hold the appointment long, for soon afterwards I had a very moving letter from his mother informing me of her dear son's death. I always thought what an excellent clergyman he would have made, though I never hinted such a thing to him, lest it should seem to savour of insult.

Another " chronic," who was also my friend, but in a much more remote degree, had, indeed, gone in for the Church, but in spite of a most commendable capacity of intellect failed to get ordained, and so went in for a medical degree, just as a man who had failed to reach the clouds might undertake a voyage to the moon. He entered the Medical course about the same time as myself, and when I left he was still pounding away at his books nine or ten hours daily ; with the result that his medical knowledge might be described by my old friend Euclid as that which has neither space nor magnitude.

He was very anxious to take out an extra course of anatomy, but by no means anxious to pay for it, although he seemed well able to. So he came to me and asked me what he should do, and, trying to look as solemn and as serious as himself, I told him that under the circumstances his wisest plan would be to plant himself at the door of the lecture room, and as soon as it was closed and the lecture began, apply his ear to the keyhole and take in every word that was uttered. This seemed to strike him as a very brilliant idea, so I enlarged upon it by suggesting that in like manner if he applied his eye to the key-hole of the dissecting room and observed all that was going on for a sufficient length of time and with a sufficient amount of attention, he would learn not only as much as would pass him, but as much as would get him honours. I am not sure whether he followed my advice, for I soon left and lost sight of him ; but I was told that for years afterwards he persisted in going up for the examination with results that seemed to indicate he had followed it, for no man ever gave his examiners more amusement or became a greater favourite amongst them.

If I remember rightly, it is told of him that his biennial appearance, like a recurring decimal, attracted the notice of the Secretary, Dr. J. Stoney, who in the fulness of his heart took him aside and said : " Mister So-and-So, I am really sorry to see you rejected so often. Don't you think it would be better to go somewhere else where the examinations are easier ? "

Mister So-and-So looked at him solemnly and replied :

" By the Lord, Doctor, no matter where you go they expect you to know something ! "

There was another case, in which, to my horrified astonishment, the advice I offered was taken. It was the case of an Arts student who failed at his exami-nation for a second year's scholarship. By this failure he was left completely " on the rocks ," for his father, a poor schoolmaster in Connemara, had stopped supplies. He came to me for advice as to what he should do, and as he was a healthy and well-developed young man, I naturally suggested the

Army or Navy. He turned up his nose at both these openings into which so many young men infinitely his superiors had entered. Seeing that he had rejected this advice, which was serious, I offered him another which was not serious, but outrageously ludicrous, and, as sure as I am a living sinner, that was the one he took. He was a Catholic, and such a devout Catholic, too, that amongst his own people he would be called a voteen and amongst outsiders a fanatic. Some time previous he had called on me and found me at dinner, which consisted as usual of a beefsteak, a chunk of bread, and a bottle of stout. It appears that that particular day was a day of abstinence on which flesh meat was forbidden—a fact of which I was blissfully ignorant. He, however, was shocked at the enormity of my transgression, and with all the severity of superior rectitude took the liberty of sermonising me very sharply on my sinful ignorance.

I remembered that incident just then, and, struck with a sudden flash of humour, suggested that as neither the Army nor Navy were good enough for him, and as work of any kind was not to be thought of, his best course would be to " turn his coat " and go back to Connemara as a Bible Reader. The Church Mission Society, of which there was a branch in Galway, would be delighted to receive him, as business was rather slack amongst them just then. They would feed him on beef, and maybe mutton, every day in the week, and would give beautiful descriptions of him as " a brand snatched from the burning " and turned into a blooming fig-tree in the garden of grace ! They would give him a new Bible with the Lion and the Unicorn pictured on the title-page ; and last, but not least, they would dress him in a white choker and a tall hat ; and after that it was very likely that some of the rich old ladies who support the good workers " in the vineyard of the Lord," would fall in love with him, marry him, and make him a gentleman for the rest of his life ! Instead of taking my words in the spirit they were meant he swallowed them as seriously as a child would swallow pap ; and without telling me, went immediately to the Rev. Mr. Austin, who was in charge of the Mission, and without more ado became what the Galway folk would call a " jumper." He was sent right off to a home called the " Crow's Nest," in D'Olier Street, Dublin, and I never saw him again. A friend and I called at " The Nest " to inquire about him, but they would give us no information. Although I never saw him nor heard about him afterwards I had no misgivings concerning his future. He would stop at " The Nest " until his father sent for him and then return like the Prodigal Son ; but I don't think he would ever again venture to lecture an acquaintance on overlooking a religious ordinance.

I observed that our " chronics " were, for the most part, solemn, serious, and hardworking men, but all of them absolutely lacking in the sense of humour, so that it was the easiest thing in the world to make stirabout in their ears without letting them feel the movement of the pot-stick. And yet when all is said and done, such men add a picturesque variety to life, and the world would be a much duller place were it not for their dulness. The overwhelming majority of them were the innocent victims of that parental vanity which flatters its possessors with the belief that their sons, merely because they are their sons, inherit enough talent to make them successful in any profession, however difficult. And so, without measuring the capacity or consulting the tastes of their sons, they thrust them into the study of Medicine, the most difficult and probably the most disagreeable of all studies unless one is born with a natural talent, or at least aptitude for it. It is the common story of the round pegs and the square holes. In my opinion the round pegs that are hammered into the square holes deserve all the pity, and those who hammer them all the condemnation.

With a vivid consciousness of my own frailties staring me in the face, I have always had a fellow-feeling for others who have lagged behind in the race on which their proud parents started them handicapped with plenty of means and unpricked by the sharp spur of necessity. If that fate had been mine I should probably have been one of the last amongst the laggards. Even as it was, although I had a rare capacity for the accurate measurement of facts and the relations of my position thereunto, I frittered away in pastime and conviviality a large portion of my time, which should have been wholly devoted to preparing for examinations. I took an active part in all the goings-on of my fellow-students, who elected me to preside at all their sport meetings, and also at the meetings of the College Debating Society, which took place every Saturday night. This mark of popularity was due to the fact that I was a senior, and, although being such, was perhaps more sociable than most seniors are. I am sure, too, that no person ever acted as Chairman who was less charmed with the sound of his own voice. This may have been the fundamental reason why I was elected so often, for I never bored a meeting with oratorical flights. No speech of mine ever lasted more than ten minutes, so that my success as a Chairman made up for my failings as an orator.

I rather regret that I entertained a certain amount of contempt for speechmaking, which was by no means akin to the fox's contempt for the grapes he could not reach, for if I had felt any sneaking regard for attaining the art I should certainly have made some effort to cultivate it, and this I never did although I had plenty of opportunities. In fact, I looked upon speechmakers as blatant humbugs, and had a wholehearted belief that the more a man orated the less he worked. I was overflown with this belief from two opposite sources, the Fenian and the Orange, which united on this point and with it permeated the atmosphere in which I was brought up—the atmosphere of Ulster—that province which has produced more workers and fewer orators than any one of the other three. This extreme view was an utterly wrong one for an Irishman to take ; for I might have known then, as I know now, that speechmaking was a very useful weapon in the hands of a people who had no other weapons left to save them from the fate of the Red Indians.

In addition to these functions I became an occasional contributor both in prose and verse to the two Galway papers, the Liberal *Vindicator* and the Tory *Express*. To me, at that time, their politics were six of one and half-a-dozen of the other. The editor of the first-named paper was so charmed with my articles that he pressed me to become his subeditor. But as he himself could hardly make both ends meet I wondered where I should come in, for I had no intention of playing the part of a Tom Pinch to his Mister Pecksniff.

What charmed him most with my effusions was

their spicy, unconventional style, and I well remember the grin with which he read aloud to his family at the breakfast table a highly edifying description of the Atlantic Hotel in my article on a Trip to the Isle of Aranmore in Galway Bay.

I have still a proof of that article, but even if I hadn't it would haunt my memory, for it runs thus :

" On landing, the first building that confronts the beholder with its stately dimensions is the Atlantic Hotel. This noble edifice is two storeys high, and is covered with a roof which is slated. It has also windows, and the door is between two of them and in the front, where one would never expect it to be. If you are thirsty, you can have a copious quencher there. Order it at 12 and you will get it at 2.30, and when you drink it you will remember it till your dying day. You can also have a dinner there of hard-boiled lumpers and fat mutton ; but if you are leaving the same day and wish to carry that dinner back to Galway, you must have your stomach lined with sheet iron."

This style tickled the jaded palates of the *Vindicator* readers. To the other paper, I contributed verses in the namby-pamby or sweetly rotten style.

Although I had sense enough to make all my contributions anonymous, I was generally suspected of being the author, and thus gained the reputation of being a trifler spiced with a dash of humour—a reputation that was no recompense for the loss of some examinations that I went in for. However, I consoled myself with the reflection that I was not such an idle trifler after all, for was I not earning from £2 to £3 a week, paying my fees with exhibitions, and making many friends ? I found not a few of them in the parents of the lads I was coaching, for the most part well-to-do business people, amongst whom the Scottish element largely prevailed ; with this element, I am proud to say, I always got on well and have always held it in the highest esteem. As Galway was one of the poorest towns in the world it would be wonderful to one who did not know their excellent qualities how these strangers managed to become prosperous and powerful in it, while many of its native citizens went to drudge in America or remained at home to nurse their poverty, deeming it as merely a preparation for their subsequent inheritance of Heaven.

My engagements were not confined to coaching lads for Matriculation. They comprised also the teaching of Latin and Botany in a young ladies' school, and private tuition to the son of the Commanding Officer of the Connaught Rangers, a boy whose health prevented him from attending school. I had no engagement that I liked better than this, for the Colonel was a bluff, genial old gentleman, who gave himself no airs in my presence and always treated me very handsomely, so I kept this engagement till my career at the College almost came to an end.

Another engagement that came to a sudden end through my own fault, if I may so call it, was that of reading to the President of the College certain nights of the week. This President was a very old gentleman, and quite a blameless nonentity, named Berwick. He was a target that received many shafts of criticism aimed at the College, for his salary and his work were as a mountain and a molehill. His wife was a mixture of fuss and philanthropy, so strictly evangelical that her talks to me always savoured of stale margarine.

The College at this time had many enemies, and amongst them there was one who became my pet aversion, although he never crossed my path, and I had never exchanged a word with him. He had been a student of the College and a graduate of the University, and having availed himself of all the benefits of the College and the kindly encouragements of the professors, he turned round and assailed them in the vilest manner. This raised my gorge to the utmost, for I had an intense love for the College and all its professors, and I felt towards this ingrate as a lover might feel whose adored mistress was vilified by a whilom suitor who had betrayed the favours conferred upon him. I concentrated my indignation in some verses which appeared in a Dublin paper, where they were complimented with the epithet " vitriolic."

This stanza is a specimen :

For all his bosh and balderdash, his bouncings and
    his platitudes,
Ferocious eyeglass and moustache, his antics and his
    attitudes ;
And other histrionic tricks, now worn rather thin,
From head to foot this braying brute belies his lion
    skin !

This portrait, which will be easily recognised by old Galway students, was drawn on the principle that any stick is good enough to beat a dog with—especially a dog that has bitten the hand that fed him.

One of the men who suffered most from this person's malignant attacks was Dr. Maguire, the Latin professor, who happened to be one of my best friends, and gave me an engagement which I found

K

very congenial and which he took good care to make profitable. He was preparing for a Fellowship in Dublin University and had to read many Greek classics within a very limited time. In order to accomplish this he engaged me to read the translation aloud whilst he glanced over the text, and this we did at his hotel, always by the light of candles, for his eyes were unable to bear the glare of gaslight. We thus read much of Plato, Aristotle, and Demosthenes, and often marvelled at the subtle intellects of the people who were able to follow the orations of the latter and catch the meaning involved in the intricate maze of words.

Few intellects of our own time, unless specially trained, would be able to act with the same perspicacity. This, however, might be explained by the fact that the Athenian intellect had fewer subjects to engross its attention than the intellect of the modern world, which ranges over such a vast number. In proportion, then, as the subjects were fewer more intellectual energy could be brought to bear upon them, just as the current of a river becomes deeper and stronger as its channel becomes narrower.

My friends at Galway included some who were neither professors, students, nor patrons, but were popularly known as " prime boys," or as they would be called in Scotland, " ne'er-do-weels." They were men whose time was divided between boating, billiard-room exercise, and lounging over a tap-room bar chaffing the affable Hebe who presided there. I will, however, do myself the justice of saying that if I associated with these men it was not for the sake of sharing their pursuits, for during my nine years career as a student I never rowed in a boat, touched a billiard cue, or paid compliments to a barmaid—not that I was any better than some of my acquaintances who did all these things, which I abstained from simply because they did not appeal to my sense of pleasure. If they had, I suppose I should have sacrificed both time and means in pursuit of them. As it was, I found pleasure in cracking jokes with these " boys," which always turned on their own personal importance, the glory of their families, and the greatness of the county families with whom they associated.

There was Dick Corcoran, newspaper reporter of lady-killing fame, who boasted that he had found favour in the eyes of the Hon. Miss Kilsheely, that beautiful daughter of the Marquis of Bohermore. Then there was Tim Belcher, a shopwalker, who informed me that on the previous night he had lost a couple of hundred quid playing cards in the Railway Hotel with his two friends, Sir Phelim O'Flaherty and Lord Drumboodle ; but it was not the loss of that trifle that troubled him—no, indeed, it was the loss of his night's sleep. Jack Lynch, the exciseman, used to give me very pressing invitations to accompany him on a seal-shooting expedition round the west coast of Ireland, as soon as he had completed the purchase of Lord Shanballymore's yacht.

These, of course, are not the real names of my acquaintances, but they are redolent of the place.

But before dropping them I am tempted to tell a story which one of them, the cleverest of the lot, told me. He was a mechanical genius, and was engaged at the College to look after the scientific instruments pertaining to the department of Experimental Physics.

It was the story of a wonderful lawsuit that occurred in the County Galway some years ago.

There were two big landowners living in the neighbourhood of the city, one called Blake and the other Joyce. Well, these two gentlemen were not only neighbours but bosom friends, and many times dined and drank together. It came to pass that one fine day after lunch the two friends took a stroll through the wood of Cranmore, in Joyce's demesne, and this stroll brought them to the edge of a pit, on which their conversation happened to turn. Joyce boasted that there was not another pit in the whole county equal in size to this one ; Blake, on the other hand, made little of it and replied that there was a pit over at Glenmore, his place, from which this pit might be stolen and never missed.

Joyce, who was awfully conceited over his pit, could not bear to have a small word said about it. Now, although Blake had a good heart and bore the pit no ill-will, but spoke only for the sake of devilment, the more Joyce puffed it up the more he ran it down. So at long and at last it happened that, without thinking on the serious meaning of his words, he said there were more nuts growing around his place in Glenmore than would fill the blooming pit, big as it was. Joyce took this as an insult to the pit and offered to bet a hundred pounds that he, Blake, could not fill it with his nuts, no, not even if he brought the bushes they grew on. Now, Blake was a hot-tempered man, and this remark was more than flesh and blood could stand ; he was also a first-rate sport and never turned his back on any man that challenged him to a bet, so he snapped at this one just as a rattlesnake would snap at a frog. They entered the bet in their note-books, signed the entries, and shook hands over it—the bet to be decided by the end of the year. It might then be the month of June, and when November came round and the nuts were ripe, Blake called out all his tenants to gather the nuts and bring them to the big pit of Cranmore, about two miles away.

Sure enough, they gathered together with all manner of conveyances, horse-carts, donkey-carts, wheelbarrows, baskets and sacks, and for three or four days, while daylight lasted, men, women, and children kept gathering those blessed nuts and bringing them over to the pit. It wasn't to say one kind of nuts, but all kinds, hazel nuts, chestnuts, walnuts, oaknuts, and beechnuts. It was all labour thrown away—they could no more fill that pit than they could fill Galway Bay. The loads upon loads that they threw into it so far from filling it lay there just visible to the naked eye, as the saying is, and the curses that poor Blake added didn't help in the least, though they might have set the pit on fire. The more they threw in the bigger the pit seemed to grow, so bye-and-bye they came to the end of their tether, which in their case meant the nuts, and they had to give up the impossible task.

Blake, to be sure, was dreadfully down in the mouth at the prospect of losing his bet, for a hundred pounds was a mighty big sum of money in those days, and people who knew the gentleman intimately whispered that he couldn't pay a hundred pence, let alone a hundred pounds. On the other hand, Joyce was not only rich, in a manner of speaking, but was a hell of a screw into the bargain ; and so he would insist on getting his bet without the abatement of a single farthing. Blake could no more raise the money than he could fill the pit, and he was too much of a gentleman to let the hat be sent around amongst his friends.

Joyce, knowing all this, put him at last into the County Court, and as there was no defence an order was made against Blake. But Blake's friends interposed, and by some means or other got execution of the order delayed and a case made out for appeal, which was to go before the high court in Dublin ; and they also engaged the very best lawyer in Dublin to act for Blake.

Well, this big pot of a lawyer came down to Galway to study the case upon the spot, and, of course, went to have a long look at the pit. While he stood looking at it, smoking his pipe and cudgelling his brains for a good face to put on his pleadings, he saw two boys sitting under a tree a-talking at the top of their voices. Wondering what their talk might be about, without letting himself be seen, he stole within reach of every word they said, and found they were discussing the great lawsuit which was the common talk of the whole county. One of these boys was Shamus O'Shanessy, the *omadhaun* of the place, and not more than forty years of age. All the neighbours looked down upon him as a creature that hadn't enough brains to carry guts to a bear, as the saying is. But, between ourselves, they were very much mistaken, for there was more in his head than a comb could take out, and if they had burned him for a fool they would have found wisdom in his ashes, for he was wise enough never to have done a day's work.

Be that as it may, he was laying down the law with a loud voice, and this, or something like it, is what the big Dublin lawyer heard him say to his companion.

" Arrah, man alive, it's balderdash ye're talkin'—
if thim lawyers wur not blatherin' idiots Squire
Blake wud hev won his case long ago. I cud hev
done it meself as aisy as cursin' if he'd put it into
my hands."

" You're a small man, Shamus, but ye hev a
mighty big mouth," says the other. " An' how in
the name iv goodness wud ye do it ? "

" Well, it's like this. I wud get up furninst the
judge and I wud say : ' Yer Hanner's glory, Squire
Blake is bound to win this case if there's law or
justice to be had in the land iv the livin'. If he
made a bet to fill this pit with nuts he is both able
an' willin' to do that same. But it nivir enthered
into the bet, no, nor even into his head, that he was
to carry the nuts to the pit—he only bet that he wud
fill it, and instead iv him bringin' the nuts to the pit,
as Squire Joyce wants him to, it's Squire Joyce's
duty, as a gintleman an' a man iv honour, to bring
the pit for the nuts, an' allow Squire Blake a fair
chance iv winnin' the bet.

" ' If yer Hanner's glory wanted a quart iv porther,
ye wud natherally send yer futman with a jug to put
it in.

" ' In this same way let Squire Joyce send his pit
over to the woods iv Glenmore an' I myself will go
bail that Squire Blake will soon fill it, but to compel
him to carry over the nuts and fill the pit as well is
neither law nor justice.' "

Now, the big lawyer from Dublin heard these
words and stamped them on his brain-pan so that he
wouldn't forget them in a hurry ; and off he went
to Dublin that same night without letting a soul
know what he had heard.

When the case came on in the Four Courts a few

days afterwards he got up and used the very same argument that he heard the omadhaun use in the woods of Cranmore.

There were no less than two judges on the bench, and they both agreed that the statement of the case was sensible and just, and decided that Misther Joyce should bring the pit over to Glenmore in order to give Squire Blake a fair chance of filling it.

When Squire Blake came back with flying colours there was great rejoicing amongst the tenantry at Glenmore, and more porter was drunk than would float the biggest hooker in Galway Bay.

When the narrator had finished I said : " Barney," for that was his Christian name, " do you wish me to believe that story." " Why not ? " said he. " Because," said I, " you're after saying that the big lawyer from Dublin left without mentioning it to a single soul, so how did you come to know it ? " " I told you," said he, " that the omadhaun, in the first place, laid it down in chapter and verse to the boy that was sittin' beside him ; well, that boy was my father, and I heard it from his own lips."

This is one of the many stories I heard from Barney as I sat with him and his cronies over our pints of mulled stout in the back parlour of Tom Hardyman's bar.

Such were some of my acquaintances. I sought and found amusement in their company, but the amusement was far from edifying, and the price I paid for it was far too high—the wastage of time and the lowering of ideals.

Besides these acquaintances I had many true friends, who, alas ! for the most part are dead and gone, but who will still live in the holiest sanctuary of my memory till death rifles that abode. They were friends in the truest sense of the word, rejoicing in my small successes and sympathising in my defeats. They were always ready to assist me with the best advice and place their purses at my disposal in case I wanted pecuniary help. Such occasions did occur, but they were few and far between, and I am proud to say never led a helper to the slightest loss.

Chief amongst these friends was an old bachelor named Sweeney, who was a Board of Works official in charge of the College repairs. He was a singularly high character, gifted with a cultured intellect and a benevolent heart that never tired in doing good. He took an extraordinary liking to me, which I fully reciprocated, and during the holidays he would insist on my spending days and nights at his house. He bitterly regretted being a bachelor, and told me it was all due to his cursed conceit when a young man. He then had the misfortune of being good-looking, and thought no woman that he met good enough to be his wife. So it came to pass in the long run that no eligible woman thought him good enough to be her husband, and he was left high and dry on the rocks of bachelordom—a fate which he bitterly deplored and urged me strongly to avoid ; and yet it was largely through his influence over me that I left Galway a bachelor.

I knew many girls there, but not one of them found favour in his sight, and I was bound to admit that his judgment was better than mine. There was one girl especially with whom I was in the habit of keeping company far oftener than a prudent regard for my prospects warranted. She was the daughter of a small farmer, who lived only a few perches beyond my lodgings, and she and some other girls used to come and play in the field opposite our door. The temptation to go out and romp with them was irresistible, so that my fellow-lodgers and myself soon succumbed to it, and as she was far the best-looking of the lot, I took on to her.

She was, indeed, an exceedingly fine-looking girl both in face and figure, and her good looks were enhanced by her simple dress, which was such as one sees in pictures of an Irish Colleen—wearing neither hat nor bonnet, but with her auburn tresses neatly tied up with a pink ribbon.

She was, indeed, a typical Colleen such as a senti-mental novelist would love to describe, especially if he knew nothing about Colleens except from their outward looks. He would go into raptures over their grace, sweetness, purity, tenderness, and all other undefinable charms that make Irishwomen so fascinating, and in all this I would agree with him.

But if he should launch forth in praise of their angelic simplicity, their noble objection to mercenary marriages, and their sacrifice of every sordid con-sideration to the voice of true love, I should say : " Hold on, my friend, how many of them have you wooed as a penniless suitor ? " As far as my expe-rience goes I have found that if our Colleens are soft-hearted they are certainly not soft-headed, and no women that I ever met with have a keener eye to the main chance. It was so with my Colleen. I cannot say that I was desperately in love, for if I had been marriage would ultimately have ensued, but I was just far enough gone to sacrifice some valuable hours every week in her company and to feel my thoughts wander to her in the midst of my studies.

I also felt considerably irritated when I found a

rival embracing and kissing her, for, of course, she had more than one string to her bow, or should I say more than one beau to her string ? When I remonstrated with her over this she very aptly retorted : " Why shouldn't I keep company with as many young men as I like ; someone of them may become my husband which you are never likely to be." " Why, then, do you encourage me ? " I said. " Because my people told me to encourage you till after your examination. If you pass that and become a doctor I will stick to you, and drop the other young men, but if you fail I will drop you and stick to somebody else." Now, these were not the words of true love, but they were the words of cold common-sense, and helped to cure me of an attachment which the wise advice of all my friends might have failed to do. With my Colleen's avowal of her strategy towards me our acquaintanceship did not terminate ; and I will anticipate the chronological order of events by stating that when I passed my examination, and returned from Dublin to Galway a full-blown M.D., the greatest surprise I received was a letter from her father congratulating me and inviting me to have tea with the family. As I had done nothing to make me shun their presence I felt it would savour of moral cowardice to refuse. I therefore went, and got a very cordial reception, and when the tea was over they put a bottle of whiskey before me, which disgusted me very much ; but I carefully avoided the snare so artlessly laid and left it untouched. I left Galway that same night and never saw the girl again, but I had a letter from her saying she would accept me if I sent her a promise of marriage in writing. To this I sent a reply that put an end to all further communication.

But to revert.   The associates and scenes of my last year at College were by no means calculated to make my exit a brilliant one or my name long-lived. I was beginning to find, like everybody else who sojourns in the City of the Tribes, that the atmosphere of pleasant indolence which pervades the place had its well-known fascinating effect upon me.   I felt as if I should have liked to live there for ever, dead to all ambition, without taking the trouble to raise myself in the world, but indolently plucking the small flowers that grew within my reach, and never hoping for anything bigger or better.   This was the life I saw all around me—the life in which my associates luxuriated—a blissful dream which I could have enjoyed had I not been perpetually haunted with the prospect of a rude awakening, and the consciousness that dawdling and dreaming would leave me nothing but a wasted life.

My happiness must consist in effort; I must struggle, not stagnate ; so I decided to drag myself out of the rut into which I was sinking and go in for every examination I was eligible for, whether I passed or no.   Three times in succession I went in for the half-degree and three times I came out rejected. On the first two of these occasions it was through my own fault, and that fault was defective preparation. On the third occasion it was through a stroke of ill-luck, for I was well-prepared, but in one of the subjects, Materia Medica, there were two oral examinations, and I left the hall under the impression there was only one.

I then returned to Galway in the face of circumstances as black as any student ever encountered. For I was not only rejected, but my pocket was empty—tenpence being all it contained—and I had to pay some eighteen pounds for the fourth year's attendance on lectures, all I had earned as a coach having been recklessly spent. I was also in bad health, and worse still, I had to meet the condolences of my friends, and feel that they began to look upon me as a hopeless " chronic," entitled to pity only.

Against all this, I had a supreme confidence in myself, and my spirits rose in view of the struggle that lay before me. As the fourth and last term of my medical course was about to open, some scholarships and exhibitions were to be competed for, so I entered the contests and won an exhibition worth eighteen pounds, which served to pay my College fees, or rather the debt I had contracted from a friend to pay them before the examination. I resumed once more my old work of coaching, and plunged into my studies so energetically that at the end of the session I not only overtook my fellow-students who had outstripped me, but came out first in Clinical Medicine and Surgery.

When it came to the last lap for the final M.D. examination I put on a spurt and no mistake. I threw up every engagement except such as supplied me with the barest necessaries of life, and I utilised every moment of my time. To such an extent did I do this that in company with a fellow-student, who was my best friend, I used to go around the hospital on Sunday and examine the patients at leisure and undisturbed by the crowd of students. This privilege was allowed me by the visiting physician, a good friend of mine. I also made friends with the apothecary attached to the County Infirmary, in order to gain some knowledge of dispensing drugs.

Although I had worked in a way that would seem to render failure impossible, when the final M.D.

examination was over I felt far from confident of the result. I was, however, so desperately determined on ultimate success, that during the few days elapsing between the last day of the examination and the announcing of results I got up every morning at four a.m., and spent all my time preparing for the next examination, six months hence, to make sure that if I failed now I should succeed then. If I failed then I was determined to do the very same thing over again, and work myself to death or madness or succeed in the end.

Fortunately, I was not obliged to pursue such a course, for I got my degree all right, and hardly felt the solid earth beneath me as I reached the goal for which I had struggled so long, and yet not so long in reality as in imagination, for after all it was only the normal four years. And if the time I spent in teaching and the time I spent in dawdling, conviviality, and courting were deducted, the four years would shrink into as short a space of time as ever transformed a student into a full-blown M.D.

CHAPTER VIII

When I had thus reached the goal of my labours, after days of exhausting examination succeeding months of incessant study, I felt as wearied and worn out as if I had been competing in a succession of Marathon races. Of this I had an ominous symptom, for on one occasion, after some slight exertion, a hundred cataracts seemed to rush through my ears, then sudden oblivion; and from that I awoke to find myself lying on the floor. No man ever needed rest more than I did, and no man ever desired it less. I was as eager to commence work in my new role as a spendthrift heir would be to enter into the enjoyment of a rich patrimony. Accordingly as soon as I got back to Galway I lost no time in writing to a medical agent in London, Dr. Baxter Langley, to get me a medical assistantship as soon as possible. I had a reply far sooner than I expected, offering one in Brynmawr, Breconshire, at £60 per annum indoor. This miserable salary, at which a skilled mechanic would to-day turn up his nose, I accepted without hesitation, and, indeed, would have done so had it been only half the amount, so eager was I to get into my new harness.

And yet in spite of all my eagerness I found it impossible to leave the dear old Citie of the Tribes without feeling a regret that I have never experienced on leaving any other place. It had been my home for nearly nine years, and on the whole a very agreeable home. Its pleasures far outnumbered its regrets and were its indigenous products, but its regrets were the products of my own conduct. Its people were more capable of winning and retaining a stranger's love than any other I have ever met with ; and if Nature had not filled me with the Demon of Unrest, and Fortune had not sent me into the world with her wooden spoon, I should have been delighted to have spent all my days amongst these kindly Paddies-go-easy, far away from the tormenting cant of the strenuous life.

No student ever left Galway College with a deeper sense of gratitude or a higher esteem for its professors than I ; and I bore away the conviction, which had been long formed and is still cherished, that if a student fails there it is entirely due to his own fault or misfortune. Though all the professors stood high in my esteem there was one who stood pre-eminently so, and that was the Professor of Anatomy, Dr. Pye. I have never met a man whom I admired more for nobility of character and cultured intellect combined with a high sense of duty and unostentatious kindness of heart. He had been a student of the College, and if that institution had never done anything but produce him it would have fully justified its existence. To lose contact with him when I had learnt to appreciate him was one of my deepest regrets on bidding adieu to the old city.

My departure took place on a Sunday, when I left by the midnight train for Dublin, accompanied to the station by my friend Sweeney, and rigged out in a new suit of clothes and a tall hat—thus sacrificing comfort to dignity for the first time in my life. Overwhelmed with the importance of my twopenceha'penny engagement I travelled with as much haste as if the fate of nations depended on my early arrival. I was, however, detained for the night at Shrewsbury—my first night on English soil and one of the most awful I ever spent. Putting up at a small hotel near the station I was in a state bordering on nervous fever, and had no sooner commenced to sleep than an endless series of images, incoherent, bewildering, and tormenting, kept rushing through my brain with the rapidity of hurricanes, and the bed seemed swarming with snakes and all sorts of loathsome creatures ; jumping to escape I awoke and found myself on the floor.

It was Nature's second demand for repose, and again I disregarded it, fortunately without any untoward results.

I did not again go to bed, but started by the earliest train for my destination, and entertained myself with taking mental notes of the people I met and the country I was passing through. The difference between these and those I had left struck me most forcibly. Here there were fewer figures lanky, bent, and badly clothed ; fewer soft blue eyes unconsciously appealing for sympathy ; fewer pinched cheeks and thin jaws. On the contrary, the majority of the figures consisted of the burly and beefy type, well-clothed, stolid and comfortable-looking, with heavy jowls, and an exasperating air of self-satisfaction that demanded respect or afforded amusement, but repelled sympathy.

The difference of the landscapes was equally striking. The one I had passed through in the west of Ireland, especially between Galway and Athlone, was flat and dreary, its mournful monotony variegated only with bogs and rocks and sparsely peppered

L

with ugly farmhouses and squalid cabins. Here, on the other hand, was a rich, undulating country, spreading as far as the eye could see like a beautiful green robe, everywhere embroidered with grand old trees, dotted with opulent and well-built farmhouses, and cosy and comfortable cottages embowered in roses and honeysuckle ; in fact, every product of Nature's spontaneity or Man's industry breathing of a comfort and content which I had never before seen. These scenes, so very soothing to my wearied senses, culminated in a singular outburst of beauty as I reached Abergavenny and the valley of the Usk, which lay before me bathed in the glorious light of a summer morning, like a veritable picture of Paradise.

From thence to my destination was an upward journey ; but the higher I ascended the uglier I found it, and the end of it was a town in keeping with this approach, and the last place in the world where one might expect a hospitable reception. The surroundings were bleak, barren, and hilly—an arena inviting summer and winter to vie with each other in proving the extremes of their forces in heat and cold. As there was no one to meet me I made my way to my principal's house, and found him at breakfast, to which he invited me, seeming much surprised at my arrival, which he did not expect till the afternoon. He lost no time in getting me initiated into the working of his practice, which was a fairly large one, consisting of collieries, clubs, and parish work, with a sprinkling of private patients.

He treated me kindly, and I really needed kindly treatment just then, for I was so shaky that I had to use both hands in raising a teacup to my lips, and I found great difficulty in measuring out the drugs. Fortunately, there was not much night work, so that I had plenty of sleep, and this, coupled with well-cooked food and absence of anxiety, soon restored me to my normal state of health.

My principal allowed the greater part of the work to fall on my shoulders, which I took in good part, esteeming it as a mark of confidence in my capacity. He invariably deferred to my judgment, never interfered with my treatment of the patients, but allowed me to prescribe whatever drugs I thought best. In this matter he and I differed widely, for, like almost all young practitioners, I was imbued with the loftiest ideals of duty towards my patients, and considered that no trouble was too great and no drug too costly to be expended upon them, whether their ailments were slight or serious. He, on the contrary, whose experience was infinitely greater than mine, had little or no faith in the efficacy of drugs—especially if they were expensive. His favourite prescription was Aqua Camph. C. Sacch. Ust. (Camphor water with burnt sugar), which, to do him justice, he would sometimes vary by writing Sacch. Ust. C. Aqu. Camph. In defence of this prescription he maintained that of the patients who took drugs ninety per cent. did not need them ; they were either slightly ill or else shamming ; and to give them drugs was only a waste of money, as Nature unassisted would make them all right again. There were, to be sure, some serious cases in which drugs might be given, even though expensive, but in his opinion such cases were few and far between—merely exceptions that proved the rule. If he had very little faith in the intelligence of his patients they had far less in his mode of treatment, for it was a common occurrence, especially amongst his pauper and club patients, when they uncorked a bottle of his medicine, to smell the contents, and, unbeguiled by the rich amber colour, pour them out with muttered maledictions.

As I had no interest in saving his drugs and earning a malodorous reputation, I invariably prescribed those I judged to be best, of which his surgery contained abundance untouched, some even mouldy.

After a few days that got me accustomed to the working of the place, he went off for a holiday and left me in full charge. Although this increased my responsibility it pleased me very much to find that he placed such confidence in me, and that I had a fine opportunity of learning to ride on the horse he left me. It was my first essay at equestrian exercise, but not my first contact with horses; for in my boyhood's days, amongst other odd jobs, I assisted an ostler in taking charge of farmers' horses in a tavern yard on market days. I had a rather painful consciousness that my first attempts at riding were by no means consistent with my professional dignity, and were calculated to inspire merriment rather than respect in the minds of profane onlookers. In order to diminish that merriment as much as possible, when I met people or passed houses I tightened the reins of my steed and reduced his slow jog trot to a walk, and wiped my brow as if I had just finished a neck-or-nothing gallop. However, with perseverance and practice I eventually became an expert rider, which afterwards proved invaluable to me.

While our colliery patients expected the doctor to treat them with consideration and sympathy, they themselves never treated the doctor on the same principle, but were often insolent and offensive in their manner towards him; of this I had a striking example before I was long amongst them. One

Saturday night a lot of them, half-drunk and completely dirty, came to our house and demanded to see the doctor. On going out I found one of them bleeding profusely from some cuts on the face inflicted in a drunken brawl. They did not ask, but ordered me to dress the cuts, just as a haughty lordling might order his flunkey. I told them to go into the surgery and I would do so ; but no, they would go into the doctor's parlour ; they were paying the rent of his house and were entitled to the best room in it, so in they went. Without feeling either cool or careful, I cleaned the man's cuts and plastered them up, and off the party went, no doubt rejoicing at their display of mastery over the doctor. When they had gone I looked at the plaster I had dressed his cuts with and found that it was blistering plaster, and I felt a grim satisfaction in imagining what a nice, comfortable and cool face my patient would have in the morning. Although, to be sure, it was only an accident, I hoped he would recognise it as an intentional punishment for his insolent conduct. He never turned up afterwards.

It soon came to my knowledge that a Galway student, who had been a classmate of mine, was settled in the neighbouring town of Blaenavon as chief surgeon to the works and pits. Being only four miles distant, I walked over to see him and received a very friendly reception. He had a most extensive practice and kept two assistants and a dispenser. It so happened that one of the assistants had given notice to leave, and my friend offered me the position at £120 per annum, or just double what I was receiving. Of course, I closed on the offer immediately, and returning to Brynmawr sent a month's notice to my principal. It was well I did

so, for I found that the latter intended to dismiss
me on returning from his holiday, as his practice
was not large enough for the work of two ; and when
he engaged me as an assistant he merely wanted me
as a *locum tenens* to take charge in his absence.   By
this trick he managed to save the difference between
my fee and a *locum's*, which at that time was three
guineas a week.   He was one of the most niggardly
men I ever knew, and I heard him rebuke a servant
for putting too much salt on the table.

During my stay with him I made a vast encroach-
ment on his expensive drugs, which the patients
appreciated so much that many of them asked me
to start a practice in opposition to him—the very
last thing I should think of doing.

We parted on very good terms, and he gave me an
excellent testimonial.   I find it impossible to let him
slip from my memory without recalling a story he
told me about a former principal of his who had a
large club and parish practice in Cardiganshire.   This
doctor had a wonderful reputation for a mixture he
was in the habit of frequently prescribing with effects
so marvellous that no ailment seemed able to stand
against it.   He kept it in a conspicuous corner of his
surgery in a beautiful porcelain keg, on which was
inscribed in letters of gold, " *Mistura Evangelica*."
The ingredients of this evangelical mixture consisted
of the rinsing of all jars and bottles that came into
the doctor's hands and needed rinsing.

From the time I left Brynmawr till I went to
Blaenavon there was a full week at my disposal,
which my late principal recommended me to spend
at Weston for rest.   Instead of doing so I went to
London, and spent it in quite the opposite way—in a
way that would delight the heart of a true Bohemian.

I visited all the sights immortalised in history and literature, and appreciated them to their full extent. Without encumbrance or care I walked from daylight till dark through the leading streets with the bewilderment of a bird set at large in the depths of a boundless forest. When I felt hungry I turned in for a meal to the nearest restaurant, and at night when I felt tired I called a halt at the nearest hotel ; never stopping two nights in the same place, as I carried no impedimenta.

Seeing the thousands upon thousands of my fellow-beings hurrying to and fro in never-ending torrents, and not knowing a single face amongst them, I was deeply impressed with the sense of my utter loneliness, and I felt that if I were suddenly cut off I should be as little missed and as noteless as a leaf that falls in the woods of autumn.

When I arrived in Blaenavon I soon learned that if my salary was doubled my work was also doubled. There was little time for rest, and still less for reading in the afternoons. When I was not visiting I was engaged in the surgery, and if haply I stretched myself on the couch for a post-prandial nap I would suddenly be aroused by an infernal jangling of the bell accompanied with a call to some outlying district. The night work was incessant, but divided between myself and the other assistant, each taking it alternately by the week. During my week of nightwork I would find sleep all but impossible, for, even when not aroused by some untoward call, I would be kept awake by the expectancy of it, and the slightest noise would throw me into a state of prolonged irritation. Under such conditions there is a strong temptation to seek relief in alcohol or morphine, forgetful of the poison ambushed behind the panacea, and that a wrecked life becomes the penalty of the transient exhilaration. Good people who have never undergone the temptation begotten of fatigue and insomnia find it very easy to blame the victim, but those who, like myself, have undergone it must substitute pity for blame.

The worst feature in our night work was the thankless nature of it, and the knowledge that the bulk of it was quite unnecessary. If only the little finger of a collier ached, or a thimbleful of recalcitrant wind lost its way in the corridors of his colon, it was " Off for the doctor immediately ; why shouldn't he come and cure me at once ? Are we not his master, do we not keep the roof over him, the clothes on his back, feed his family and provide him with a horse when he ought to tramp around li¹⁻ᵃ the rest of us ? " Such thoughts seemed always present in the minds of the colliers, and were sometimes uttered in my presence, because, I suppose, I was far from formidable looking and unable to reply with a kick, as my principal would have done had he heard them ; for he was a tall, powerful young man and gifted with a temper that would stand no nonsense. I could only shape my feelings into unutterable maledictions, not on the tyrannical colliers, but on that man or body of men who first put the collier's foot on the neck of the doctor by introducing contract practice.

It was, indeed, possible for the assistants to retaliate in some mild ways for this abuse of night-work in its more flagrant forms. They seldom did so, but showed superhuman magnanimity in the sacrifice of their resentment. Yet on rare occasions the bearer of a needless call would be put to considerable inconvenience in this way : If he had come from a distance of several miles on a wet, wintry night he would instal himself in a nice comfortable chair in the waiting-room in front of a cheerful fire, which was kept burning through the night, and there he would remain till the doctor rode off to see the patient and returned to send the medicine. Now, if the doctor found the call an unnecessary trial of his patience, or got treated in any sort of a high-handed manner, he would, as in duty bound, prescribe for the patient, but leave the prescription behind. On his return he would find the messenger dozing comfortably before the fire, and he would then be asked for the medicine, but the doctor would tell him it was no part of his duty to carry prescriptions. He had left it at the patient's house, and the messenger would have to return there and bring it to the dispenser, who lived a long way off, and get him to come to the surgery and make it up and deliver it to him. In such cases the patient generally did without the medicine, and would be quite well next day.

Gratitude was rarely expressed amongst these contract patients, and, as they never felt the payment of medical bills, medicines and medical services were never properly valued by them. If they recovered from an illness it was accounted a stroke of good luck, but if they did not recover the fault was put on the doctor. I remember spending a night of heartbreaking anxiety attending a poor woman who was rapidly sinking from uncontrollable hæmorrhage. While I was doing all that it was possible for a medical man to do she died in my hands, and as I left the house I was assailed with shouts of " You butcher " !

If I obtained no gratitude, which after all may be doubted, I certainly did my very utmost to win it, and I honestly believe that I deserved it. I was not only very careful and attentive to my patients, but was sympathetic as well. I was always able to imagine in what way I should like a doctor to act towards me if I were in their position, and in that very same way I felt it my duty to act towards them, and expect no gratitude beyond that of my own conscience.

The two and a half years that I worked in Blaenavon were amongst the hardest in my life. I had known what hard physical work was, and I had known what hard mental work was, but here was a combination of the two such as I never before had experienced ; and yet these years were fruitful both in profit and in pleasure. The profit was professional and consisted of enlarged experience and skilled proficiency in the treatment of medical and surgical cases, as well as an increase of confidence in my own powers which nothing but a still wider experience could shake. The pleasure arose from feeling the acquaintanceship between me and my employer ripen into a very warm friendship, which became a charm that lightened my toil and allured me to remain in that limbo of labour far longer than I intended. That friendship would have continued till this day had it not been cut short by his untimely demise some years afterwards, which left me with an unforgetable regret. But, surely, I am wrong in saying it was cut short when it remained with his widow and children and will end with another demise only.

The monotonous round of toil that constituted my life in Blaenavon was broken by few incidents worth recording.

Once I spent a month in Dublin practising operative surgery under that eminent surgeon, Sir William Stokes, when I succeeded in getting the degree of

M.Ch. or Master in Surgery, which I esteemed very highly, as it is one of the very hardest to win. On the same occasion I got the diploma in Midwifery. But to anticipate and have done with these titles, I was made M.A. in the following year, and that, too, in my absence.

I had, indeed, a fortnight's rest, if rest it could be called, when I was laid up with diphtheria caught from some of my patients. And still another fortnight's rest, for so I considered it, when I was told off to attend some smallpox patients and strictly prohibited from doing anything else.

Another incident was a tilt over a matter which touched me very keenly, with the chief director of the works, the all-prevailing potentate of the place. This great man, who, if I remember aright, was afterwards parliamentary candidate for North Monmouthshire, delivered a lecture in the Workmen's Institute to a crowded audience, which happened to include myself. I forget what the subject was, but at any rate in the course of his remarks he said that all the races of mankind were fit to govern except the Irish and the Negroes. If I had been struck across the face with a whip I could not have been more hurt and insulted ; but at the same time I felt that if I had jumped up and got into an argument with him I should probably make myself ridiculous, knowing that I was a bad speaker at the best of times, and that in a temper I should speak worse than ever.

I, therefore, nursed my anger until I got back to my rooms, when I wrote him a letter I shall never forget. In that I branded him in bald and brutal phraseology both as a liar and a coward—a liar because Irishmen had proved their governing capacity,

not only in all parts of our own Empire, but in all
parts of the civilised world wherever their lot was
cast. I supported my statement with a long list of
well-known names. To prove that he was a coward
I pointed to the fact that he took advantage of a
meeting packed with his own people to insult the
one isolated Irishman who happened to be present,
though I do not now think that such was his intention. Furthermore, I added that speeches like his
were more mischievous, misleading, and provocative
of bad blood than anything ever said by those
agitators whom he deprecated so much, and about
whom he seemed in a state of brute ignorance.

In reply to this letter he sent me an apology, or
rather the abortion of an apology. He and I never
again ran across each other, but for many years my
letter was preserved in the office of his Company,
as a curio, I suppose, in the art of invective.

On my departure from Blaenavon, I went to
London, took lodgings in Huntly Street, off
Tottenham Court Road, and put myself in communication with several medical agents to procure
me work as *locum tenens*. I succeeded in getting as
many appointments as kept me busy for about a
year and a half, when I gave up working for others
and started on my own account.

My work as " *locum* " was by no means difficult,
and the succession of changes which it entailed
charmed me with their novelty, forming, as they
did, a delightful variant from the monotony of the
life I was accustomed to. They comprised an
engagement with a most estimable Quaker family in
Staines ; one with a Welsh doctor at Ashby de la
Zouche ; one with a Scottish doctor at Finsbury
Park ; one in Bristol at a sixpenny dispensary ; and

a very prolonged one with an Irishman in the Ogmore Valley. Now, why should I mention the nationality of these employers? Well, because this question was brought very prominently before me in seeking engagements. I was almost invariably asked : " Please state your nationality and religion," and I invariably replied : " Irish and Roman Catholic," and invariably received a polite rejection, but no Scotsman or Welshman ever put such a question to me. About this time when I was negotiating for the purchase of a practice in Luton, Bedfordshire, the vendor asked me : " Are you an Irishman ? " I answered in the affirmative, and he then said : " But you are not a Roman Catholic ? " " Yes." " Well, then," said he, " it is useless for us to go any farther into the business ; for the patients there might tolerate you if you were an Irishman only, and not a Roman Catholic ; or they might tolerate you if you were a Roman Catholic only and not an Irishman, but I'm afraid they would never stand a combination of both."

In saying I was a Roman Catholic I am sure Roman Catholics would repudiate me ; for I looked upon all religions with an impartial eye and practised none. But I made it a point of honour to say I was a Roman Catholic because it was the religion of my mother ; and I looked upon any Irishman who would change it for another with the same loathing that I would look upon a human skunk who would kick a poor relation out of his house for the sake of an enemy's bribe.

For this wave of racial and religious prejudice sweeping over England just then, the Phœnix Park murders, which had recently occurred, were the chief propelling power. With the unreasoning force

of virtuous indignation good people were so carried
off their heads that they judged everybody belonging
to the country and creed of the murderers to be
more or less responsible for the crime. But if their
neighbours had judged them in the same way anent
murders committed by their own criminal lunatics
they would have felt grievously wronged, and yet
there would be as much reason in the one judgment
as the other.

At that time a medical friend of mine was thus
addressed by a lady patient: "You're a Scotchman,
are you not?" "No," said he, "I am not."
"Then you must be a Welshman." "No, I am
not a Welshman." "Well, what might you be,"
said she. "I am an Irishman," said he. "Well,"
said she, "I suppose you cannot help that. There's
good and bad from all countries." And so she
poured balm upon his sore.

Whether I deserved it or no I was generally
reckoned among the "good," for I tried to assimilate
myself to those I mixed with, and I found them
all good people whom I hold in kindly remembrance.
I could have spent my life very pleasantly knocking
around in this fashion, but I began to feel it was
high time to set about making a practice for myself.
I was no longer a spring chicken, but a tough old
rooster, much further on the shady side of thirty
than I cared to reckon. Instead of purchasing a
practice, I decided on finding an opening somewhere
and creating one: for, I am sorry to say, I had no
scruples about poaching on other men's preserves,
and felt I would much rather be a wolf than a lamb.
Now, where was I to find such an opening? After
a brain-cudgelling process I hit on a rather ingenious
plan. I took the Medical Directory and compared

the ratio of the doctors to the population in all the chief towns of Great Britain, exclusive of London, and found that this ratio was lowest in Preston, Barrow-in-Furness, Oldham, Wolverhampton, and Cardiff, and I decided on visiting each of these towns to see how the land lay. Cardiff was the first of these places that Fortune placed in my way, and having carefully studied its pros and cons I decided to go no farther.

My acquaintance with Cardiff was made in this way : I got an engagement from Dr. Thomas, of Maesteg, to manage a practice in the Ogmore Valley, and to get there from London I had, of course, to pass through Cardiff. But let me pause at this Ogmore practice. It was the most disagreeable I ever worked, though by no means the hardest, and the only redeeming feature about it was the kindly attitude of Dr. Thomas, whose occasional visits were like gleams of sunshine breaking through a gloomy atmosphere. I had to put up in a collier's house, with his wife to wait upon me and serve me with the food of the family ; and I had no one to talk to except my host and hostess, and their children after school hours. The surroundings, as far as I can remember them, though perhaps my memory is prejudiced, were dreary and mountainous, like a happy hunting ground for lost souls. I felt as if I should soon be numbered amongst these, but I saved myself by going to Bridgend and purchasing copies of Keats and Wordsworth, and thereby imbibed refreshment more delightful than wayside inn ever afforded to a weary traveller. I did not even pause at the " Excursion," but drained that long draught to the bitter end—a feat which I have never known anyone else to perform.

Much against my will, I was detained here several weeks beyond the terms of my engagement, for the place had a bad reputation, and Dr. Thomas had great difficulty in finding my successor. But at last he did find him in the person of an elderly apothecary, whom I pitied sincerely. I never left a place with more pleasure, and I am sure that pleasure was reciprocated amongst the miners. As an example of what they expected from me—and did not get—they claimed that it was my duty to walk around every morning from house to house and inquire at each house if my services as a doctor were required, and thus save them the trouble of sending for me ! It appears that my predecessor, a Scotsman named Robertson, did this—a Scotsman above all men !

On my way back to London I stopped at Cardiff ; saw its possibilities, and concluded that I could find no better sphere for my future labours.

However, before entering that sphere I went back to London and took the most important step in my life—I got married ! I had long contemplated this step, for I was utterly alone in the world, and shuddered to think of the fate that lay before me if I ever reached old age in that state which is mocked with the name of single blessedness, when in reality it is single cursedness. I imagined myself at the mercy of some harpy of a housekeeper, if I became rich enough to keep a house, or else an inmate of some frowsy boarding-house, where I would be a nuisance tolerated only for the sake of a weekly remuneration.

The door of Destiny that sends forth the most important issues in the lives of men sometimes turns on a very small hinge. It was so in my life—if any event in so insignificant a life can be called important.

One fine afternoon I happened to be strolling some-where near Vauxhall Bridge, when I saw tramcars labelled " Camberwell " pass me. This name suddenly drew my recollection to a letter of intro-duction to a lady there, and searching my pocket I found the letter. Having nothing better to do I decided on seeing what this letter would lead to. Mounting one of the cars I landed at the address given, and might describe the result by changing one of the words of Cæsar—*veni, vidi, victus fui.*

The honeymoon was spent in Boulogne, and the second day after I returned I found myself in Cardiff, where I arrived as complete a stranger as if I had dropped from the planet Mars.

With Cardiff as my home since then I have passed some three and thirty milestones on the rough high-road that stretches between the cradle and the grave. It seems a long distance, and yet, owing to the variety of pursuits with which it was diversified, I hardly felt its length. It was like a long distance, walked amongst the sights of a city, appearing short in comparison with the same distance walked on a bare country road.

M

CHAPTER IX

When I started in Cardiff as a general practitioner, I started on lines that made failure impossible. I got a map of the town, as it then was, and marked the most central spot which the penny tram-fare rendered accessible from all the other parts. Taking a small shop there I turned it into a surgery without allowing my professional dignity to stand in the way of prospective advantage. It was a smart stroke of business in which I stole a march on a Bristol doctor who was on the point of coming and doing the very same thing. Smart as it was, it was nothing to boast of, and I don't think I should start in the same way again.

During the years I had been managing other men's practices I carefully noted all the mistakes they were making, and the disastrous effects of these mistakes upon their practices, and so I was resolved to avoid them. The most prevalent mistake that I had noted was stinginess in the matter of drugs. I have, indeed, been in surgeries where large numbers of patients have been ministered to from a supply of drugs that would hardly be worth five shillings. There is nothing more maddening for a conscientious assistant or *locum tenens* than to find that his patients want medicines which he cannot give, unless he pays for them out of his own pocket at the nearest chemist's. I have sometimes done so when the patient was poor ; at other times I have given a prescription when the patient was able to pay the chemist, but in either case the proceeding, disguise it as I would, must have been prejudicial to the interest of the practice I was managing.

One of the worst offenders I ever knew in this respect was, as might be guessed, a double-barrelled professional, who during the six week-days attended as a doctor to the bodily ills of his patients, and on the seventh ministered to their spiritual wants in the chapel of which he was pastor. No ; he was not a Welshman. But even in Wales I have sometimes been almost overcome with nausea in some surgeries on comparing the ostentatious profusion of sacred texts on the walls with the paucity of useful drugs on the shelves.

On the rock that might be labelled " Spare the drug and spoil the patient " it was my fixed determination never to get wrecked. Accordingly, as my practice grew and my output of mixtures increased *pro rata*, I wrote direct to the German manufacturers of the most costly drugs I used in order to ascertain if they would send me those drugs direct. They replied in the negative, but sent me the address of their agents in London from whom I could obtain them in large quantities much cheaper than from the wholesale druggists. I availed myself of this information, and also got my spirits, ten gallons at a time, from the distillery at a price much below the ordinary wholesale. I was told by some of my substitutes that I was only wasting valuable drugs by prescribing such large quantities, but I replied that drugs are only wasted when given in doses too small for their full therapeutic effects. I observed, too, that all the medical men I had worked for sent out their mixtures in bottles containing sixteen doses ; I, on the contrary, never put more than eight, six, or even four doses into a bottle, for I had noticed a custom common amongst patients on getting a bottle of new medicine, especially if it was cheap, to throw it aside if it did not seem effective after the first or second dose, and with looks of disgust remark : " This stuff is no good." In the sick-room I have often seen half-emptied medicine bottles lying about.

I also made it a point never to put peppermint into a mixture, for no matter how good the mixture might be the patient almost invariably says on smelling it : " Oh, this is only peppermint water ! " and I insisted on my dispenser compounding each mixture on an open counter and never behind a screen in the conventional fashion, about which I had heard many unfavourable remarks. I did my visiting on entirely new lines by insisting on getting paid for each visit as I made it, and never making a second one unless I was sent for. As an assistant I had heard many malicious and unfair complaints about doctors making unnecessary visits in order to pile on the agony in the shape of a long bill ; and I decided that such complaints should never be made about me. There were, indeed, occasions when I found it quite impossible to adhere rigidly to that rule. If, for instance, I were called to some poor man or woman suffering, say, from pneumonia, and I got paid for the first two visits, was I to abandon that case when I knew that further payment was impossible ? No, a thousand times no. I would continue visiting till the case ended one way or other, without asking or expecting fees. If I should happen to receive any in the long run it would be an agreeable surprise ; but I never bothered with booking or bills, and every night my pocket contained my day's earnings.

I always knew well those people who wanted to elude this rule of mine, and, as the saying is, " to put their finger in my eye." Most of them lived in villas and seemed highly respectable, and would almost invariably tackle me in this way : " Now, doctor, we want you to take particular care of this case ; you come and visit just as often as you like and your bill will be paid at the end, no matter what it is." I always heard this with a grave face and an inward smile, and always replied : " I don't keep books or send bills, but I make it a rule to get paid for each visit. You'll pay me now and send for me again if you want me." Sometimes this was done and sometimes it wasn't, but in the latter case no medicine was sent. I observed, too, that such people never appeal to a medical man's charity, but always speak to him in a patronising sort of way as if they were doing him a mighty big favour by employing him ; and he, poor soul ! believes he is very lucky in getting their names on his books. When he sends in his bill he will probably learn that they have shifted their address, and he and the landlord may shake hands on finding themselves equally " bilked."

By acting as I did I am sure I had less trouble than most medical men, and though my fees appeared lower than the average my receipts were quite as high, if not higher. But this result was obtained only by the vaster amount of work that I performed, for no doctor could have worked harder whether by day or by night. However, I found infinite pleasure in my work, inasmuch as all my earnings went into my own pocket, for was I not my own master ? And above all I revelled, O, how I revelled, in the glorious privilege of being independent. I was in a position to make my patients feel that I was doing

them a favour by attending on them, and not that
they favoured me by their patronage.

In aiming at success I considered that my first
object should be the earning of a reputation, and
that I should not rashly attempt to build a fortune
without first securing a good foundation on which
to raise it ; calculating that when such a foundation
was laid the edifice would rise rapidly and securely.
Is it not Thackeray who says, that every man starts
life as a blank cheque which he can fill up for any
sum he likes, be it ten or ten thousand pounds, and
the world will accept him according to this valuation ?
I put a low figure on my cheque, intending to add
to it gradually as the edifice of my fortune grew ;
but the initial figure was a supreme mistake, for it
brought me work that was out of all proportion to
its remuneration, and being underpaid was under-
valued.   In this I was largely the victim of circumstances, for in my early days I was accustomed to
work for such poor wages that the fees which a rich
man's son would consider small appeared to me
quite large.   In fact, ten shillings would seem as
large in my eyes as a pound in the eyes of another,
and many years of labour elapsed before I was able
to free myself from the bondage of this illusion.

I made another mistake in calculating the attitude
which the medical men of Cardiff would assume
towards me ; for I had learned from my experience
of other places that the relations between their
medicals were not always based on brotherly love,
and least of all towards a stranger.   Such, I judged,
would be my own lot amongst the medicals of Cardiff
for coming amongst them as an interloper and a
poacher, just as a hawk might enter a farmyard ; I
expected no mercy and was quite conscious I deserved

none. It was, then, an agreeable surprise to find
they were far more magnanimous than I imagined,
for though my tactics must have been very provoking
to their sense of conventional dignity they seldom
showed it ; and their leading members always met
me in consultation on friendly terms. Looking back
at my long medical career in Cardiff I consider myself
very fortunate in having had my lot pitched amongst
such honourable and high-minded colleagues as I
met there, colleagues in whom I found some of the
best and dearest friends of my life.

This career extended over more than five and
twenty years of arduous and anxious work which I
attended with the regularity of an automaton moved
by faultless machinery. Throughout all that time,
with the exception of Sundays and annual holidays,
I was never a day off duty ; and every Sunday was
spent walking or driving in the country, at least when
the weather permitted. These Sunday trips were not
only beneficial to my health, but were sources of
infinite pleasure. The scenery surrounding the city
or within easy access of it was the most lovely I had
ever seen, and even now, after having visited many
of the finest parts of the civilised world, that opinion
remains unchanged. Oh, ye glorious Sunday outings,
how brightly ye shine through the mists of memory !
If I could only get my youth and strength renewed,
and backed with a modest income of ten thousand
a year, I would make every day in the week like
unto you. I would not swoop through the country
like a hurricane, flattening fowls and purveying for
the coroner on a forty horse-power motor, which
allows nothing to be seen except the road in front
and devours that almost as soon as it is seen. No ;
I would stuff my pockets with " the needful," take

my walking-stick, and meander along at the rate of three miles an hour. I would observe every object worth observing, and stop at every bit of beautiful scenery until I had satiated myself with its charms, and then I would pass on and retaste the pleasure in the discovery of some newer attraction. At the end of the day I would turn into the best quarters I could find ; order the best dinner they could cook ; and having smoked my last pipe and drunk my last whiskey and soda I would thank Heaven for having given us such a beautiful world and wonder why so many people should grumble.

For many years I used to take a month's holiday in the summer and spend it in as near an approach to this ideal as I could afford, in some one of the numerous localities that make our islands the most beautiful summer resort in the world. Although my income was rather below the modest sum I have mentioned, and I sometimes had to exercise a little ingenuity to keep things square, I believe I saw more and had more enjoyment than many people could procure for ten times my expenditure. Throughout my walking holiday I never made a hotel my head-quarters if I could find a farmhouse or cottage where they would receive me ; and in this respect I was sometimes very lucky.

During one of my visits to the English Lake district, in strolling from Ambleside around the head of Lake Windermere, I spied a beautiful old cottage some distance from the highway, clothed with clematis and woodbine and well screened with trees. I was quite enchanted with its beauty and seclusion, and wondering if I could become its guest I approached, inquired, and, sure enough, was accepted and made happy for about twelve shillings a week—surely the scenery of that district glorified with the names of Wordsworth, Coleridge, and the " English Opium Eater " was never enjoyed at a cheaper rate.

In the Isle of Man, where I went next, I was equally lucky, for arriving in Douglas one afternoon I was shocked at the noisy and disorderly crowd that was turning the place into a pandemonium. Though I like, above all things, to see people enjoy themselves according to their own sweet will, this enjoyment was more than I could stand, yet I thought I could stand anything. Then turning my back on Douglas and its promise of a sleepless night I started for Port Soderick, a little seaside place which the guide-book said was " a haven of rest." So far from being so I found it worse than Douglas, if worse were possible, for every hotel and lodging-house in the place was crammed with trippers, and it was impossible for me to get a bed. As it was then getting late I went back to the station in a state of desperation and told my story to a porter. He pointed to a light away in the distance and advised me to try there and perhaps I should get a night's shelter. So there I went through lanes that seemed interminable and found a farmhouse where, in the best sense of the word, I was taken in. I stopped there a week, going out in the morning and returning at night when my day's walk was over. At the end of the week when I asked for my bill they told me to pay whatever I liked, and if I could not afford anything it would make no matter. I did not take advantage of their hospitable offer, and they welcomed me to stop there as long as I liked, and complimented me by saying that my company was ample recompense. They were English folk who had come from Manchester, and I mention this fact with pleasure to let my Keltic brothers know that we do not monopolise the virtue of hospitality.

Tramping in Scotland I found emptied the purse quicker than tramping anywhere else in the United Kingdom. I should, however, be sorry to say that the Scottish hotelkeepers and their servants are extortioners, but I will say that they seemed to labour under this amiable delusion that all travellers who came amongst them were millionaires in disguise, and should be treated as such when settling the hotel bills. Yet I was once, strange to say, treated as a mortal of ordinary means at a place called Corpach, from which I made the ascent of Ben Nevis. My hotel was less a hotel than a farmhouse, kept by a sonsie housewife called Mrs. Macpherson, who took me for one of her own countrymen, at which I felt mighty pleased, for I knew she would not then venture to treat me otherwise than fairly. My surmise was right, for I never was better treated or charged less. I may here remark that when I visit any town in England or Wales I try and find out the hotel frequented by Scotsmen, and there I put up, not only because I like the company, but I am sure of getting the best accommodation at the most moderate charge.

I made a special pilgrimage to the beautiful land of Burns, who is one of my idols in verse and one of my aversions in prose. He has been charged by the " unco guid " with many sins, but I could gladly forgive them all except his letters in high-flown English. On my visit to his natal cottage I was told an amusing story by the good lady who has charge of the museum connected with the cottage. Some time previous to my visit she had been showing a party of English visitors over the museum, and evidently did it in so satisfactory a manner that one of the ladies of the party wishing to pay her a compliment on leaving remarked : " I am sure, ma'am, you keep this place much tidier and cleaner than ever Mister Burns did when he was in charge of it ! "

But after all France was my favourite country for walking ; nowhere else except perhaps in Switzerland have I been able to obtain so much comfort at so cheap a rate. After a delightful walk through the romantic region that was once Provence, redolent with troubadour memories, I turn in to a wayside inn, order dinner, and get served with an omelette, a chicken, and a bottle of good old wine, all for about three francs, or half-a-crown in English money. But if one turns into one of our own wayside inns all one can get is cold beef and pickles, which are my abomination, a bottle of beer, and a chunk of cheese as indigestible as a paving-stone. And while paying the highest figure for this repast you are treated with looks that suggest you are getting it for charity. I have never heard foreigners speak a good word of the wayside inns of Britain, and I have heard Americans speak of them as abodes of horror to be carefully avoided —pitfalls that spoil the pleasure of travelling in a beautiful country.

Although I have lived in all the four provinces of Ireland and have seen all that is worth seeing in the country, there is no part of the British Isles wherein I have walked less. During my long residence there I was too busy to walk far for pleasure or sightseeing, and in my latter years while on casual visits I had to content myself with travelling by rail or by sidecar—the latter being the most uncomfortable vehicle

I ever experienced, not even excepting the Norwegian *stolkjoerre*. It is a veritable survival of the unfit, and therefore I suppose it is patriotic to stick to it.

My travelling in Ireland as a pedestrian having, as I said, been rather limited, my experience of the country's wayside inns must necessarily be the same. But such experience as I have had enables me to say that I preferred them to those in England. The food was simpler, and never spoiled with the inevitable pickles, cheese, and raw vegetables ; and drink much better than beer could always be obtained. I have, indeed, remarked that Irish drink, especially Irish whiskey, is very like the national character ; it is never mediocre, but always good or bad, and when it is good there is nothing in the world above it, but when it is bad there is nothing in the world below it. Whatever the food lacked in variety was made up by its abundance, which amounted to downright extravagance. It seemed to be the established rule for each guest at each meal to leave his plate half-full of the food he was eating—a habit that always filled me with disgust, and I should like to have compelled those who acted in this manner to have eaten the leavings of other people's meals, just as they expected other people to eat theirs. In explanation of this custom I was told that hosts, in order to show their hospitality, would keep overloading the plates of their guests, and the latter never left the plates empty lest it should appear they hadn't had enough ! I hope this custom of hospitality gone mad is now extinct, even in spite of its good intention

There was one very pleasant commodity in which the wayside inns of Ireland excelled all others that I have ever visited, and that was civility. The landlord in each would overwhelm me with the most amusing stories, both old and new, both home-made and imported, would post me in all the details of his business, and take me into his confidence as if I were a lifelong friend. And when I settled my amazingly small bill with him he would receive my few shillings with as much gratitude as if I were bestowing a fortune upon him.

One topic I always found taboo, and that was politics, which amongst the people who are the keenest politicians in the world I thought very singular. If a stranger expresses a political opinion, no matter how harshly it grates upon their feelings, they listen with respectful silence and try to change the subject. I have known some of my Unionist friends who travelled in the south and west of Ireland return with conviction that all the people there were of the same opinion as themselves, thus mistaking polite reticence for assent.

For many years my annual holidays consisted of trips that made me acquainted, however slightly, with all the countries of Europe except the Balkan States ; and I also contrived to extend my journey to Tripoli. As my holidays never exceeded six weeks I made the most of my time, and being fairly well conversant with the history, if not with the languages, of the countries I visited, they teemed with interest, information, and amusement—the people I met with contributing to the latter.

My first visit to Norway aroused within me a love for the sea, quite equal to my love for the land with all its beauties ; and henceforth my annual holiday generally included a sea trip which introduced me to some part of the world hitherto unknown.

My next trip was to the Mediterranean on a Cardiff tramp—a mode of travel which I prefer to that provided by any floating hotel that ever crossed the ocean. On a tramp I was not bored by the insipid loquacity of passengers, nor disgusted with their snobbish airs, neither was I required to organise entertainments in which I had no more heart than a skeleton would have in the Egyptian feast at which he was planted.

As doctor on passenger boats it was considered part of my duty to do this, but, I am glad to say, I never did it; for much as I like to see people amuse themselves, I draw the line at becoming a purveyor of their amusements on compulsion, and a ship's surgeon who does this adds nothing to the dignity of his profession.

If the meals on a tramp are not so conducive to gourmandising as those on a liner they are wholesome and digestible; and taken in company of the captain and officers they are seasoned with the conversation of interesting and intelligent men. Another great advantage that I found on the tramp was freedom from the nuisance of perpetually drugging passengers. When a doctor's services can be had gratis it is wonderful what a number of people become ill—so seriously ill that advice without medicine is no good— so they must have medicine, and still more medicine !

Fortunately, there is always plenty of black draught, Epsom salts, and castor oil on board, and the doctor, who of course has the temper of an angel, can always recompense his patients for the trouble they give him by treating them generously with these dainties.

From each of these holiday trips I was wont to return with a fresh stock of mental and bodily energy, and plunge into my work as a ravenous glutton would plunge into a long-delayed banquet. But just as a surfeit may await the glutton, a breakdown may await the worker, and such would have been my fate had I not foreseen and avoided it.

My work had grown to unmanageable dimensions —for six hours daily, with the exception of Sundays, I used to attend in my surgery and prescribe for seventy or eighty patients at least. Besides this I would make about twenty visits between noon and evening, and when I would return home at night I should probably find several new messages awaiting me, and off I would start again on another round. When the day's work was really finished I was so jaded and worn-out that I felt as if I should never get up again once I lay down ; and when I did lie down it would be to a sleep restless and broken with anxious thoughts about my patients, and whether I had done all that was possible for those in a dangerous condition ; and my mistakes, real or imaginary, would flit through my brain like a procession of black phantoms.

Year in year out for nearly a quarter of a century this was my daily routine—a routine that absorbed all the energies of both mind and body, and turned me into an animated machine for taking in small fees and turning out prescriptions, just like a penny-in-the-slot arrangement. I became so quick at it that the patient had no sooner stated his case than I had his prescription ready—diagnosing him as it were intuitively. I had no time to write down names and addresses or to copy prescriptions ; but I had an excellent memory on which these facts were faithfully copied and seldom faded.

It was not until after many years that I grew dissatisfied with becoming a machine working at high pressure, even though it was bringing an income that promised to make me a wealthy man. I had an uneasy feeling that I was probably working away my life for the sake of a fortune I should never enjoy, and at the same time putting a temptation to idleness in the path of those who should inherit that fortune. With these reflections, strengthened by the old saying : " What is the world to a man when his wife is a widow ! " I decided on retiring as soon as possible.

I was forced to execute this decision far sooner than I anticipated, for although I worked as a machine I was, after all, not a machine of iron, but of flesh and blood, and even as that very flimsily put together. Although I saw clouds gather which portended a storm that would have left my poor frame a complete wreck, I continued my work in spite of the menacings until I was stopped by a sudden illness which seemed very unfortunate but eventually turned out to be a blessing in disguise. This was a sharp attack of influenza, on which diabetic symptoms supervened, rendering me very shaky. However, I decided to hold on to my work for another two years, but according to the best medical opinion in South Wales it would be absolutely impossible for me to do so ; and I had to choose between retiring from work at once or retiring from life in the near future. As I always found life well worth clinging to I decided on the former alternative, which was accompanied with the proviso that I should take things easy and spend my winters in a warm climate.

These conditions were by no means harsh, and by faithfully fulfilling them I have been enabled to " husband out life's taper " ten years longer than I expected.

My rest was simply a change of activity from the practice of medicine to the pursuit of travel spiced with journalism, and sometimes mingled with a renewal of professional duties as ship's surgeon. But before touching on this new phase of my existence I shall briefly advert to the position I long filled as a political leader of my countrymen in the city of my adoption.

CHAPTER X

From the suppression of the Fenian movement in
1867 till I left Ireland in 1880 I took no interest in
politics except to treat them with that cynical contempt which is often the result of ignorance, but
still oftener the result of intellectual vanity, flattering
its possessor that he has a soul too exalted to take
interest in matters that engross the vulgar. With all
my reading I quite overlooked the fact that politics
are the outcome of that interest which people take in
the management of their country, and the amount of
such interest is the measure of their liberty and
progress. If we compare the histories of the East
and the West this is the very first fact we are impressed with. In the most backward countries of
the East there are no politics, while in the most
advanced countries of the West the atmosphere is
alive with them. They are the business of free men,
not of slaves and savages who relegate the business
of their country to the unquestioned control of
despotic authority.

I judged all politicians to be a lot of advertising
self-seekers endowed with lungs of leather, brows of
brass, and voices like the bull of Bashan's. Seeing
that I had never met with politicians this judgment
was about as valuable as that of a critic on books
he had never read. Under the impression that the
best service a man could do his country was to mind

his own business, and let the business of the country mind itself, I jotted down the following stanzas :

> By force of talents, largely writ
>   In their own calculation,
> Some men believe that thay are fit
>   To manage all the nation !
>
> To hear such men their trumpets blow,
>   Expound and criticise, Sir,
> You would believe they were in tow
>   With all that's great and wise, Sir.
>
> But if you turn them inside out
>   It will be quickly found, Sir,
> That every thing they set about
>   Has tumbled to the ground, Sir.
>
> Give me a tongue of modest tone,
>   A clear-eyed soul behind it,
> A little business, all my own,
>   And sense enough to mind it !

These were the opinions with which I landed in England. What, then, changed me ? Reading of the articles upon Ireland that were appearing in the London papers, with one or two honourable exceptions. These articles seemed to me the foulest weapons ever issued from the armoury of Race-Hatred. They were steeped in venom and wielded with an arrogance and ignorance that defeated their object, for instead of tending to unite the two nations into an imperial homogeneity they tended to widen the gulf between them and foster mutual hatred and distrust. They were very effective means for recruiting the ranks of rebellion in Ireland, and I had often seen them quoted for that purpose. I am sure I interpret the feelings of my countrymen correctly when I say that an injury hurts them less than an insult, and that the latter rankles in their minds long after the former is forgiven and forgotten.

But I am equally sure that the latter result has been obtained by the beneficent policy of late years, which has turned all our old rebels, like myself, into staunch supporters of the British connection ; and if I still take a very small part in politics it is with the object of strengthening the new relationship. I recognise, too, with much pleasure that the London Press, with one exception, has dropped much of its hectoring and lecturing, its bullying and browbeating of Ireland and her people, especially since the commencement of the present war. But at the time I speak of, what should any honourable Irishman do but stand up for his people so foully dealt with ? and this, I am proud to say, is what I did.

When I came to Cardiff the " United Irish League," or " National League," as it was then called, had not been introduced into the town, but was started immediately afterwards at a meeting at which I was present. Although I was a stranger and absolutely unknown to any of my own country-people I suppose my position as a doctor gave me some claim to recognition, and I was unanimously elected Vice-Chairman of the branch that was then organised. The Chairman was the leading Irishman of the place—a man of wonderful ability and highly popular, being endowed with the gifts that are said to distinguish our race—eloquence, humour, and geniality.

I attended the meetings for some time afterwards,

and as the Chairman did not do so, I always occupied the Chair. Finding me there on one occasion he made a very flattering speech in my favour, and proposed that I should take his place as Chairman, seeing that he should be unable to attend regularly. This was agreed to, and so I became Chairman—a position which I filled for at least twenty-five years, and one that brought me into contact with many eminent Irishmen, and modified the unfavourable views of politicians that I previously held.

It is for the sake of recording my impressions of these men that I have here introduced my own political experience, which otherwise could interest nobody.

The first event that brought me into public notice in Cardiff was the arrival of Michael Davitt, who came here to lecture soon after his release from Portland Prison. The Nationalists who organised the meeting had the bad taste to ask the Catholic Bishop to attend, but instead of doing so he sent a stern refusal, and strongly denounced Davitt for some utterance which he was alleged to have made against the Pope. Owing to this circumstance, as well as the unpopularity of the Irish cause at that time, there was great difficulty in finding a Chairman for the meeting. All the representative men of the Irish, both lay and clerical, were approached, and all refused. As a last resource they fell back on me, and though their offer was thus stripped of all compliment, I readily accepted it. I felt proof against any assaults of public opinion, and was rather pleased to show my contempt for the censure that frightened my compatriots—for was I not an old Fenian, hardened to that sort of thing ?

Accordingly, when Davitt came I took the Chair,

and for the first time in my life spoke in public
before a huge audience. I took the precaution of
having the speech well prepared and delivered it
without a hitch. It was conciliatory in tone, was
well-received, and reported without the omission of
a word. Instead of making me enemies it made
me friends even in Conservative circles, while Davitt
and I formed a friendship that only terminated with
his death.

In my opinion Davitt's death was the greatest
loss that Ireland sustained in the nineteenth century,
the only loss comparable to it being the death of
Thomas Davis some sixty years previous. His personality was the most magnetic I ever knew—its
power to attract the love of friends and respect of
enemies was irresistible. When I say enemies I
mean political enemies, for I am sure he had no
personal ones.

His patriotism was supported by a faith that never
doubted and a courage that never faltered, and his
sincerity and earnestness impressed all who approached him with the conviction that here was a
man prepared to back his principles with his life.

He nurtured no conceit about his own powers,
nor jealousy about any of his colleagues ; and never,
I am sure, uttered a mean insinuation against friend
or enemy. He had the rare judicial capacity of
viewing a controversial question from the opposite
side, and giving his opponents credit for being
actuated by motives as good as his own, however
mistaken they might be. Of this I had a very forcible
example on venturing in his presence to speak rather
harshly of Clifford Lloyd, a resident magistrate
notorious for his severity. He said Clifford Lloyd
was a man who did his duty fearlessly and honestly ;

and though his idea of duty was mistaken, it was conscientiously believed to be right, and therefore ought to be respected. Some years afterwards I spoke to him about the Meath election, for which he had been unseated on the ground of undue influence used by his clerical supporters. " Well," said he, " I was not only unseated but was made bankrupt, and yet I have no fault to find with the judgment ; it was perfectly just, but I was no party to that influence ; it was exercised without my knowledge and shocked me when I knew it."

It was this broadminded and generous tolerance that won him such a high place in the esteem of his opponents, so that even some of those from Ulster informed me that if all Home Rulers were like Michael Davitt they too would be Home Rulers, for it was impossible to conceive him harbouring any sinister designs against them.

The greatest achievement of Irish patriotism during the past fifty years has been the bringing together of the British and Irish democracies, transforming their secular feud into friendship, and substituting for their prejudices and animosities the solidarity of common interests. In this great and beneficent work Davitt was the pioneer, and T. P. O'Connor a worthy collaborator who is still carrying it on to a successful issue. Davitt never came to South Wales without honouring me with a visit, and his friendship amply repaid me for any odium I had incurred or sacrifices I had made in the National cause. I might, indeed, say of him as was said of somebody else that to love him was a liberal education, to which I will add it was a moral education as well.

Another distinguished Irishman of whom I can speak with first-hand knowledge, seeing that he too honoured me with a visit, is John Dillon, honest John, as they call him in Ireland. Although no one who knows " The Party " would suggest or believe that any of John Dillon's colleagues possess less honesty of purpose or sincerity of conviction than himself, none of them have these qualities stamped on their appearance in so pronounced a manner. It would be almost impossible to study his face and manner and hear him speak without feeling that these qualities are the key-note of his character, and fill him with the spirit that burned in the martyrs of old. His lofty features, not like ordinary features moulded in flesh and blood, but apparently chiselled from old ivory, are suffused with a tinge of sadness intensified by the dark eyes in whose depths it is easy to see noble enthusiasm and sublime ideals. The entire look, seeming to wander so far away, is that of a saint or hero touched into life from the canvas of Velasquez and ready to suffer or fight on behalf of any good cause that offered.

It was through this likeness that one of his colleagues, unfortunately afflicted with an itch for providing fun for his country's enemies, dubbed him the Knight of the Rueful Countenance, quite forgetting that the name Thersites might have been well given in exchange.

The only appropriate name for John Dillon would be the Irish Bayard.

I never met Mr. Healy, though I was one of his earliest admirers, and if I afterwards changed my mind the fault was certainly not mine. It happened through a speech I heard him deliver to an Irish audience in Liverpool, which at first was disposed in his favour, but before he sat down was almost to a man dead against him. The speech, as usual, was an attack on his colleagues—not a straight-forward frontal attack, but sly, insidious, and snakelike—in fact, every word resembling the hiss of an enraged cobra. It turned all my admiration of the speaker into bitter resentment, which I am glad to say time has modified or turned into pity.

I have since met with many excellent men who were friends of Mr. Healy, and I gladly admit he must have many excellent qualities who was able to win such friends. Of these friends there was one whom I had the pleasure of knowing well, and whose memory I hold in affectionate remembrance. This was his father-in-law, the late T. D. Sullivan, for some time Lord Mayor of Dublin, and for all time poet laureate of the Land League and one of Ireland's foremost lyric poets. He was one of the most charming personalities I ever knew—a pure patriot, a gifted orator, and a raconteur overflowing with humour, of which he has left an immortal sample in his popular ballad of " Murty Hynes."

If my old friend T. D. S. experienced the neglect and ingratitude that so often falls to the lot of the Irish patriot, I am quite sure posterity will do ample justice to his merits.

The next Irish leader whom I had the honour of meeting in Cardiff was James Francis Xavier O'Brien, who passed away before the consummation of his country's hopes, but left a name that will stand amongst the best and bravest in her history. His death was a loss to his country second only to Davitt's, and was, perhaps, more felt amongst the Irishmen of Great Britain than amongst those else-where on account of his position as their General Secretary ; for thus coming into closer contact with him they were better able to appreciate his character, which would be the more highly esteemed the closer it was seen. It was, indeed, a modest character that shrank from noising itself abroad by mere platform performance, but embodied its ideals in silent and strenuous action. He had been the leader of a Fenian regiment in the rising of '67, when he captured and disarmed a police force and burned the barracks after rescuing the women and children—an act for which he was complimented by the judge who sentenced him to death—commuted to penal servitude for life. When liberated some years afterwards he happened to be a passenger on the boat which then plied on the Corrib between Galway and Cong, when whom should he meet as a fellow-passenger but the judge who sentenced him, and now not only recognised but greeted him most cordially and invited him to lunch !

He was entirely devoid of rancour, either personal or political, and took his imprisonment in good part, telling me he was as well-treated as could be expected. In the House of Commons he was deeply respected, and by none more so than by members of the party he opposed. And yet with all his broadmindedness and amiability he was a strict disciplinarian, and as he never spared himself in the duties of his department he expected that all who served in his ranks should do the same.

Of this he gave a notable example in Cardiff when he suppressed a branch of the organisation and severely censured its president, a popular parish priest, for having taken a donation of £12 from a municipal candidate who was opposed to the principle of Home Rule. In fact, he told me that if a priest went wrong he deserved more censure than a layman, for he ought to know better.

In the discharge of his duties, whether painful or pleasant, he was most ably seconded by another very dear old friend of mine, John Denvir, who for many years filled the position of Chief Organiser to the Irish League of Great Britain. In this capacity Denvir travelled over the length and breadth of England and Wales, visiting every city, town, and village wherein a handful of his people were known to be located—an indefatigable torch-bearer spreading amongst them the light of Ireland's gospel, and seeking no other reward than the consciousness of having done his best for his country and his people ; and high as is the esteem in which they hold his memory it is by no means commensurate with the services he rendered them as a publicist and organiser.

Although I have met many men in the Nationalist ranks more prominent than this old friend I have met very few more able, and certainly none whose memory I hold dearer.

Charles Stewart Parnell while in Cardiff did me the honour of becoming my guest—an honour which I afterwards regretted, for it disillusioned me about my favourite idol. I met him with feelings bordering on adoration and left him with feelings bordering on disgust.

Parnell impressed me as a high-handed autocrat who secretly despised the homage of his followers, and considered that they only honoured themselves by worshipping his Mightiness. As Wilkes, the arch-demagogue, once said to a lady who was complimenting him on his principles : " Madam, I hope you don't take me for a Wilkite." In like manner I could conceive Parnell saying : " I hope you don't take me for a Parnellite." Instead of speaking kindly of the Party who had placed him on his high pedestal, and who would, as the saying is, have " put the hair of their heads under his feet," he spoke of them with what I conceived to be ill-concealed contempt ; and when he referred to Michael Davitt as " that fellow Davitt," I felt a revulsion of feeling against him which lasted many a long day afterwards.

It is true there was a difference between him and Davitt just then on the question of Land Nationalisation *versus* Peasant Proprietorship ; but even that would not justify such an expression, which Davitt would never use against him, nor, indeed, against any other opponent. It was certainly not the utterance of a democratic leader, but rather the utterance of an arrogant aristocrat against a democratic leader. On the morning of his departure from my house he displayed the same spirit in the most motiveless piece of mendacity that I ever witnessed. Before he left his room I received a telegram from the Irishmen of Newport, in Monmouthshire, asking me what time he would arrive there, in order that they might welcome him at the station with the usual display of banners, bands, and cheering crowds. I went into his room and asked him for the information required, when he replied : " Those fellows have wired to me already this morning, and I have sent them full information, so take no notice of their message." " But," said I, " what am I to do with this prepaid reply ?" Said he, " I'll use that for something else." To say I was thunderstruck at this would not half express what I felt, seeing that he had only dressed, and not left his room, and had neither received nor sent off any telegram. I inwardly prayed : " Heaven help the people who worship this man, and what an infernal lot of fools his worshippers are." But even so, the meanest of them just then rose higher in my esteem than their idol.

The mystery and mendacity with which Parnell was wont to enshroud his movements no doubt exaggerated his importance in the eyes of his followers, but may not have been done with that motive. But it was done so often, apparently without any motive, as in the instance I witnessed, that taking his family history into consideration, it might be taken as a symptom of latent insanity. Another symptom pointing in the same direction was his intense suspicion of danger, for in my presence he pulled a revolver out of his breast pocket and placed it on his bedroom table. This seemed to me a very queer proceeding, but he excused it by saying that he need not carry the thing as he was now amongst friends.

The impression I then formed of Parnell has been long since changed, and I prefer to judge him by his great qualities rather than by his small traits. His magnificent moral courage and indomitable will were united to a womanly tenderness, a sympathetic humanness, which must have won the hearts of all who knew him intimately.

As an instance of this I remember that my daughter, who was then a child some three years old, brought him a rose from the garden. He seemed delighted with the flower and stuck it in his buttonhole, and not only took the child on his knee and kissed and fondled her, but made her his chief companion while my guest. I doubt if any man ever bore a more loving heart under a hard exterior. But the hard exterior was only the crust over the volcano under which it was possible to see the fire that flickered ever and anon from those wonderful brown eyes which it was impossible to look into without feeling their irresistible magnetism—a strange compound of indomitable will-power and kindly sympathy.

In the days of his downfall he reminded me of Milton's Satan :

> All is not lost, the unconquerable will
> And study of revenge, immortal hate,
> And courage never to submit or yield !

He informed me that his family originally came from Cheshire in the reign of Charles II. and therefore were long enough in the country to have become thoroughly Irish, although there was no Irish blood in them. I presided at the meeting he addressed in Cardiff, which was one of the largest I ever saw in the city.

In the course of his address he treated his audience to a " wheeze " which for splendid audacity surpassed anything I ever heard on a public platform. It was to the effect that in his quarries in Wicklow he employed a lot of Orangemen as labourers, but had occasion to engage a number of Welshmen also. Then it came to pass that when the latter arrived at the quarries the bloodthirsty Orangemen assaulted them in the most brutal manner, and would surely have murdered them had not the Catholic workmen rushed to their assistance and saved their lives. As I was in the Chair I had, of course, to listen to this with a serious face ; fortunately, there were no hecklers present.

I accompanied him to Newport, and on the way asked him his opinion on the General Election which was then, 1886, going on. He said we should win many seats in England, but should lose some in Scotland owing to the religious bigotry of the people. In this forecast he was entirely mistaken. We lost seats all over England and gained a few in Scotland.

When we got into the railway carriage on our way to Newport he ensconced himself in a corner and was soon buried in a newspaper ; I followed his example with another paper, and not a word passed between us. Indeed, during the whole of his stay with me I carefully avoided boring him with my conversation. At the dinner, which he shared with me and Sir E. J. Reed, a friend of mine was present —a very dear old friend, sterling Nationalist and devout Catholic. Parnell happened to observe that he was a Protestant, upon which my friend remarked : " But I hope you won't die one, Mr. Parnell." Parnell at once flushed up and said : " Certainly I will, most certainly." The same gentleman remarked how pleased he was to see the Catholic Bishop present on the platform at our meeting, but Parnell remarked rather drily : " He didn't seem a bit comfortable." Being a staunch Protestant he was not indifferent in religious matters, and told me he should be sorry to see the Irish people follow the example of the French.

His Protestantism was one of the chief sources of his strength, for no spiritual power could frighten him with the command : " Thus far shalt thou go and no farther." He was the only Irishman of the century who had a fair chance of effecting a union of the Orange and Green—the foundation on which Ireland's future must rest. It appeared to me that between him and the clericals there was no love lost ; they regarded him with jealousy and suspicion, and he regarded them with contempt, sometimes, but not always, thinly concealed under a mask of respect. They confronted each other like two anta- gonists with their hands on the hilts of the swords which they hesitated to draw, each waiting till the other would give him an opening. A high-placed ecclesiastic said to a friend of mine : " Parnell is now a great man, but if he makes a false step we'll crush him with a heavy foot." I asked one of Parnell's lieutenants about the result of such a conflict. " Well," he said, " the Present is with the clericals, but the Future is with us."

When the great split took place I led the opposition against him in Cardiff, both from my republican dislike of his autocratic attitude, and my personal dislike of his mystery and mendacity. It is noteworthy that while he had an immense following in Ireland, the Irish in Great Britain, almost to a man, went against him—a fact almost entirely due to the encouragement we saw given to him by the Press of our enemy. If he were alive and the same crisis to occur again, I don't think I should adopt the same attitude, for the longer I contemplate his character and career the more I admire his great qualities— his indomitable courage, his unbending will and lofty dignity, which dignified the Irish cause, so long associated with whimpering and whining.

The fidelity with which he clung to his fatal passion and the audacity with which he braved public opprobrium might indeed savour of madness, but it was the madness of a noble mind. I hope, nay, I am sure, that all his great qualities will live in the memory of future generations of his countrymen when all his faults and failings are forgiven and forgotten.

Another public man with whom I once disagreed as I had done with Parnell was Sir E. J. Reed, M.P. for Cardiff for so many years. He was one of the most versatile men I ever had the pleasure of knowing, and if he never had taken to politics at all might have left a distinguished name either in science or literature. He was richly endowed with humour, wit, eloquence, and geniality, and was always willing to do a good turn to his political enemies, no less than to his friends. As far as my small capacity extended I supported him both publicly and privately through all his contests except once, when Parnell issued his impolitic manifesto in favour of the Conservatives. A strong friendship arose between us, for though I might have some doubts about the soundness of his political principles I had nothing but admiration for his personal qualities. But at last there was a rupture between us owing to a letter he wrote to *The Times*, giving advice to Mr. Gladstone on Home Rule which I, in common with many of his constituents, considered a most insidious attack on that measure. I denounced him very strongly for this apparent tergiversation, and accused him of being embittered with disappointment. He completely turned the tables on me by stating that I judged him in a way he would not expect from an old friend, and in a way he would never have judged me. In fact, he made me feel sorry for the hard things I had said about him, and so I resolved to make atonement if the opportunity ever arose. Sure enough, the opportunity did arise.

At the last time he contested and won the seat, I was, as usual, President of the United Irish League in Cardiff, and at our meeting on the eve of the election it was decided that we should write to Sir E. J. for his views on Home Rule. We did so, and the reply was far from satisfactory. It abounded in expressions of good-will for Ireland and her people, and great praise for his Irish friends and constituents, but contained neither pledge nor promise of support for Home Rule. It was a phantom beautiful to look

o

at, but offering nothing that one could grip, and when the secretary read it over to me privately I told him it would never do, and that it must be thrown aside, and a deputation of our members appointed to wait on him and get a definite answer. This was agreed to, and I was nominated on the deputation, but judging that the Irish electors might consider me too much of a Liberal and too little of a Catholic to represent them, I refused the position and suggested that the most popular Irish priest in Cardiff, whom I shall call Father Blank, should take my place. This was likewise agreed to, and so the deputation waited on Sir E. J. Reed, and were accorded a most gracious reception, which put all the members into a good humour and completely threw them off their guard. He tickled them with straws and sent them away delighted, without giving them the slightest pledge of support. The priest whom I nominated, Father Blank, was so carried away with this balderdash that he wrote a letter to the Cardiff papers recommending the Irish and Catholic electors to support Sir E. J. Reed, because he had not only pledged himself to Home Rule but to Catholic Education as well. About two days after this letter appeared I received a very urgent message from Sir E. J. to call upon him at his hotel. I obeyed the call and found him in a state bordering on despair.

He showed me a huge pile of letters that he had received from his Nonconformist supporters, stating that if he did not immediately repudiate Father Blank's manifesto regarding Catholic Education they must withdraw their support from him. " Now," said he, " you see what a dilemma that d——d old fool of yours, Father Blank, has got me into. If I do not repudiate him I shall have all my Nonconformist supporters against me, and if I do repudiate him I shall have your people against me, so that it seems to me I might as well retire at once." " Well," said I, " as my representative has got you into this fix I shall do my best to get you out of it." But he shook his head despairingly and said : " I don't see how it is possible." Struck with an idea which some might call brilliant, and some might call shady, I went to my office and wrote him the most scathing letter that any candidate ever received. I told him that he was only deceiving the Catholic electors, that I had carefully studied the answer he had given our deputation, and that it contained no promise whatever of support to Home Rule, and, if possible, still less for Catholic Education; that it was only vague declamation to mislead simple-minded men, but could not mislead me ; that I quite saw through it, and was so much disgusted with it that I would not support him, and withdrew my promise of standing on his platform and signing his nomination paper. When I read this letter to him, which many a man would have knocked me down for writing, he only smiled and said : " Now, what do you want me to do with this ? Do you wish me to publish it ? " " By no means," said I, " for if you do, there's not an Irishman in Cardiff will vote for you. But get it lithographed and send a copy of it with your disclaimer to each of those correspondents who has written to you for a repudiation of Father Blank's manifesto. They might not believe your repudiation, but they will certainly believe my letter."

Sir E. J. acted on my advice, and as a result got both the Nonconformist and Irish Catholic support, so that he was returned by a very respectable majority.   He acknowledged his obligation to me, and we renewed our old friendship, which lasted till his death, even though he changed his colours, or rather came out in his true colours, for I loved the man quite as much as I distrusted the politician.

At the same time I tried, but tried in vain, to indoctrinate my supporters with my views, which must have appeared very unorthodox in their eyes. I invariably impressed it upon them that Ireland was a Nation and not a denomination ; and when it was suggested that the Catholic Bishop should be asked to one of their banquets, I proposed that the Protestant Bishop should also be asked, so that the League should act consistently with its non-sectarian programme.   The study of the Past in which they were so much absorbed received from me but little respect, and I always inculcated that Life is a race in which those who would win must keep looking before them, not behind.   Whatever admiration I bestowed on Ireland's Past was confined to Fionn and his pagan warriors and bards, and not to Patrick and his saints.

On being told that every Irishman who neglects to have his son taught the Irish language is a traitor to his country, I replied that every Irishman who neglects to have his son taught a trade is a traitor to his country ; and that it matters little what language a man speaks if he lives a slave and dies a pauper.   Though long accustomed to swallow flummery and soothing syrup, my people resented the change of diet that I recommended far less than I expected, for I never allowed any hostile outsider to traduce them to my knowledge.

In spite of my outrageous heresies our people put up with me, and I was able to inspire some few of them with the belief that if ever the League got into a tight corner I would not turn my back on it. But if I did not turn my back on the principles of the League I turned my back on my position as Chairman.

It came about in this way that a lot of young men had recently joined, and these were the products of a lop-sided education, which is the curse of so many, making them more prejudiced and intolerant than those who have no education at all. The worst of the lot was their leader, a foxy-headed firebrand of a priest, who puffed them up with the idea that they were God's chosen people ; and if they wished to remain so they must carefully give the cold shoulder to their friends who were leprosied with the deadly sin of being neither Irish nor Catholic. When they were getting up a banquet for Saint Patrick's Day, our National festival, they passed a resolution in my absence that none but Irishmen should be admitted. At the next meeting I vehemently protested against this idiotic course, and pointed out that it was a direct slap in the face to the people from whom they earned their living, and amongst whom they had so many well-wishers and friends. I told them I would on no account sit at such a banquet, neither would I any longer act as Chairman to a body of men capable of making a proposal so abjectly fatuous. So I not only retired immediately, but set about getting up another banquet to which all our friends, English Welsh, and Scottish, were invited, and that, too, irrespective of their politics or religion.

I spoke to some of our parliamentary leaders about my action and they warmly approved of it. No further attempt was ever made by any body of Irishmen in Cardiff to exclude friendly outsiders from their banquets, and though often asked I never again, except for a few weeks, took office in the National ranks. But though absent in body I was with them heart and soul, and as a private individual always did my very best for the Irish cause, and without seeking popularity obtained it. I have, indeed, always held the opinion that a man who goes in for politics, especially Irish politics, for the sake of popularity does not deserve to get it.

Small as the sphere of my political labour was, it extended beyond Cardiff, and at one time included both Newport and Merthyr, by which towns I was twice elected a member of the Executive Council, and on each occasion was opposed by Cardiff—an illustration of the old maxim that a prophet is without honour in his own country. That, however, is not to be wondered at when the prophet bears the character of a crank, as I did.

As their representative I once had a deputation from the Nationalists of a neighbouring town to learn how they should act in a quarrel they had with their priest, who set himself up to become their political dictator in opposition to their political principles. I told them the means of dealing with him were very simple, and lay entirely in their own hands : let them cut off the supplies and starve him out of the place ; after all, he was their servant, not their master ; they paid the piper and had a right to choose the tune. The reply was if they did so he would cut them off from all religious benefits and let them die like dogs. I then told them if they were afraid of that there was no use in asking me or anybody else what they should do : they put the whip into his hand and must blame themselves and not him if he used it upon them.

All the enemies I made and all the opposition I

encountered were due to the fact that I was credited with being strongly anti-clerical. Now, this was quite true, but only in a limited sense, for my anti-clericalism went no farther than opposing clericalism in the domain of politics. I respected the cleric, be he priest or parson, so long as he confined himself to his clerical functions and administered spiritual consolation to those who stood in need of it, but when he plunged into politics I considered his influence positively pernicious on whatever side he chose to use it. Such influence makes no converts, but repels rather than attracts, and if I were a parliamentary candidate and could afford the expense I should adopt the Machiavellian policy of secretly hiring some clerical orators to support my opponent. I say this well knowing the harm that priests, animated with the very best intentions, have done to the Home Rule cause in Ireland by perpetually crowding its platforms and thereby keeping away Protestant sympathisers. In like manner I know how some Protestant ecclesiastics, both bishops and parsons, discredit the Unionist cause by their blood-curdling appeal in support of it. My aggressive attitude on this matter made me many enemies amongst my own people, but the Nationalists of Newport, Mon., were an exception. I could always reckon on their support, and was always honoured with their confidence. For many years I have been Vice-President of their branch, and often represented them at our annual conventions. I have never done so without feeling happier from the renewal of old friendships, and always felt more patriotic from the contact with the spirit that pervaded these reunions.

It was, indeed, always a pleasure to see my old friend, T. P. O'Connor, figure on these occasions as the presiding genius, and display such wonderful tact and talent in the management that it was impossible not to feel " here is the right man in the right place." I have often seen him, like Virgil's Neptune calming the angry waters, get up, and with an imperious wave of his arm evoke harmony from a discordant storm of words.

That I shall be a component, even a silent component, of such reunions in the future is possible, but hardly probable. But, be that as it may, these reunions, together with my whole political experience, remain green places in my memory on which I shall ever look back with pleasure ; and if I had to live my life over again, and were confronted with the same combination of circumstances, I should pursue the very same course and endeavour to win the very same friends.

Before closing the portrait gallery of my political compatriots, I am tempted to include two specimens who neither well nor wisely played minor parts in what has been very aptly called " The Irish Tragedy of Errors." These two men were O'Donovan Rossa and P. H. Pearse, of whom one sacrificed his liberty, the other his life, for the sake of those principles that aimed at benefiting their country, but fell far short of the intended aim.

O'Donovan Rossa, whose real name was Jeremiah O'Donovan, changed for the territorial title of a Gaelic chieftain, was a big, burly man with a broad, open face that always wore a genial expression, so that if you met him without knowing him, you would take him for a simple, good-natured farmer, and this was really his true character. I judged him to be a most harmless individual whom no one could know and take seriously, although he took himself quite seriously, for he was not overburdened with the gift of humour, and still less with the gift of self-discernment. On his first visit to London after his liberation from penal servitude he called on a medical friend of mine, an extremist like himself. This friend wrote to me that Rossa would visit Cardiff amongst other towns on a lecturing tour. Would I receive him ?

I consented on account of the Fenian days when he loomed large in my youthful eyes. Then Rossa himself wrote to me in a style that reminded me of the French Revolution, for he did not address me as " Sir " or " Dear Sir," but as " Citizen James Mullin," and I was charmed with his contempt for conventionality, and am sorry I did not preserve his two letters. I was asked to preside at his lecture, but declined with thanks, for although I looked upon his vapourings as less mischievous than amusing, I reflected that the public here might take a different view and I should find myself placed in a very false position.

His lecture, however, was a very harmless affair, and consisted of a recital of his sufferings as a convict, which he did not minimise, interspersed with snatches of Gaelic songs. He professed friendly feelings towards the English people and reserved his hatred for the English government of Ireland. But a man more incapable of translating his words into action I could not imagine. He told me that when he went to New York after his release he opened the " Chatham Hotel," which was so well-patronised by his countrymen that he was soon sold out and left penniless. " But it was all my fault," he said, " for I never asked my countrymen for payment, and I am sure they would have paid me if I had asked them." He struck me as a man of childish simplicity, not, indeed, without vanity, but without every quality that would make a man more dangerous to others than to himself, and I fancied how admirably he would have posed as a conspirator in one of Gilbert and Sullivan's operas.

I was introduced to P. H. Pearse at the Pan-Keltic Congress in Cardiff, to which he had been sent as a delegate from the Gaelic League in Dublin, if I remember aright. He was a young man, and neither in appearance nor in manner a revolutionary or even a political partisan, and the very last man whom I should have taken to be a leader in rebellion. He struck me as being an idealist with his head in the clouds, and he looked the part to perfection. He was completely obsessed with one idea, and that was the cult of the Irish language, which he considered a panacea for all the ills that Ireland suffered from. In fact, I sat beside him at a lecture in which he told his Irish audience that if they only learned Irish it would save them from pauperism, lunacy, and crime, which prevailed amongst them in a relatively larger degree than amongst their fellow-citizens. Whether this statement is true or false I am not prepared to say, and he gave no evidence in support of it ; but he evidently believed it, and uttered it as the advice of a friend and not as the reproach of an enemy, though this latter view was that of the audience owing to the rather tactless way in which he spoke. For this reason his speech had not the effect he intended.

At the public meeting of the Congress he spoke for nearly two hours in Irish without being able to see that he wearied the audience, of whom not more than three or four understood a blessed word of what he said. Moreover, he inadvertently caused me some chagrin, for I had written a song for the occasion, which Dr. Parry, Professor of Music at the University College, had set to music, and arranged for the audience to sing, and copies printed at my expense were distributed amongst them for this purpose. Other items were also crushed out, so that the murmurs of disappointed vanity were wide if not loud. On the next day I took him and a Belfast friend to visit Llandaff Cathedral, when we had a discussion on the religion of the ancient Irish, which he maintained was under the papal jurisdiction the same as to-day. I asked if that were so why should the Pope, Adrian IV, issue a Bull, confirmed by his successor, Alexander III, handing over Ireland to Henry II, empowering him to convert the natives to the Roman authority and compel them to pay Peter's Pence. He replied that the Bull was a forgery and never issued by the Pope. I asked him for proof, but beyond referring to some internal evidence he gave none, so we dropped the subject, each, I suppose, more steadfast than ever in his own opinion.

Pearse's political views seemed to me to be quite mediæval, and he had no hope for Ireland until she revived her ancient language and got rebaptised in one of her holy wells, as a dreamer of '48 put it. Like many others of his unfortunate countrymen he was unable to differentiate between facts and fancies, and fondly imagined that the hard realities of the actual world would cease to exist in presence of his highly coloured imaginings, and that one bird in the bush was worth two in the hand. As with so many Irish idealists whom I have met his political and historical horizon was limited to his own country. As far as I could learn he had never travelled and was unable to estimate the drawbacks under which

Ireland laboured in comparison with other nations. He was a man of one idea, and such a man is always dangerous, if not to others, to himself, even though their motives are most pure and patriotic. That such were the motives of Pearse I have no doubt, and it was therefore with deep sorrow that I read of the poor fellow's execution, and felt that it would inspire thousands to follow his example. Now, I am sure that all " right-minded " people, who are always more or less narrow-minded, will say that if a man breaks the law, or leads others to do so, he deserves punishment commensurate with his offence, and most probably the bloody Assizes of Judge Jeffrey and the butcheries of Cumberland after the battle of Culloden were made to appear justifiable by this reasoning. Nowadays, however, the opinion, the wise and beneficent opinion, is growing that reformation, not retribution, should be the aim of those who are empowered to administer the law, and more especially should this be so when the motive of the law-breaker is altruistic. What benefit does the community derive when the punishment of one law-breaker leads a thousand others to follow his example, and this is precisely what the execution of Pearse and his associates has done ?

The whole sad course of Irish history teaches that capital punishment for political crimes acts rather as a stimulant than a deterrent, and when Irishmen are inspired with that spirit, which is known as patriotism all over the world, no matter what England may call it, they will not discard it through fear of death, but will consider the glory of a hero or martyr cheaply purchased by the sacrifice of a few uncertain years of life. With this opinion I quite agree, but at the same time I believe that the hero or the martyr should be judged not alone by his motives, but also by the issue of those motives.

During my subsequent years of office as President of the Cardiff branch of the United Irish League nothing worth mentioning occurred. I regret to say I performed the duties of my office in a rather per-functory manner, and, in the summer at any rate, seldom attended the meetings, which were held on Sunday, the only day on which I had an opportunity for my favourite enjoyment of rural scenery—an enjoyment I never sacrificed for the sake of any duty, either political or professional.

I often, indeed, felt conscience-stricken on com-paring my own selfish conduct with that of my brother-Nationalists, who Sunday after Sunday, year in, year out, sacrificed their only day of rest to meet in a dingy room to discuss the affairs of Ireland, and contribute their hard-earned pence to a cause that meant no material benefit to them. The vast majority of them had never seen Ireland, but were descendants of the human flotsam that was cast on the shores of Britain by the great famine waves that swept over the ill-fated country in the middle of the last century. All the ancestral passions, prejudices, loves, and hates were transmitted to them, and seem to have been intensified in the transmission by their system of education, which is so much concerned with the Past, and by their intermarrying, which segregates them from the rest of the community and prevents the influx of new blood and new ideals. It, therefore, happens that their brogue is as mellifluous as ever I heard in " Cork's own city," and their Catholicism as fervent as I ever witnessed in a Connemara chapel, while their patriotism, which brings no profit, either present or prospective, has no equal in the modern

world, even though the patriotism of the modern
world, as evinced by its every-day sacrifices, has
reached a height never before attained.

It was impossible to mix amongst such men and
not get infected with their spirit, which was a moral
tonic to my utilitarian nature.

CHAPTER XI

In the last months of my life as a medical practitioner the menace of an early collapse became acute. Diabetes, like an insidious enemy, was stealthily commencing to sap the outworks of life's fortress. I became so shaky on my legs that I should have found it difficult to walk a furlong and impossible to walk a mile. The gums shrank from the teeth, leaving the latter no *locus standi*, so that they dropped out, to their credit be it said, quite painlessly. I was tormented with an everlasting thirst and a painful sense of fatigue that no rest could alleviate, and this, doubtless, was due to the disturbance of the balance between repair and waste of the bodily tissues, when the latter process was much in the ascendant, and I was daily getting thinner. I was, in short, becoming a physical wreck rapidly drifting on the rocks.

The mind, too, seemed to sympathise with the body, and sank into a state of hebetude that blunted the understanding, dimmed the imagination, and rendered me almost as incapable of mental as of physical exertion ; while I was also getting impatient over trifles, and sometimes felt as if my temper were likely to become my master, which hitherto had never been the case.

In these accumulating evils I recognised Nature's demand for rest ; but not the rest of the bedroom or armchair, which would have meant my transformation into a human vegetable—the most melancholy of all endings, and to me, at any rate, far more abhorrent than sudden collapse in the midst of activity. The rest that I sought should be attended with change— the latter being the greater desideratum of the two.

I was lucky enough to find a purchaser for my practice, which otherwise I should have been obliged to leave gratuitously ; and then without the interval of even one day's rest at home I started to travel the day after I gave up possession. I booked for a circular tour on the " Prince Line " of steamers, starting from Manchester by the Ship Canal and proceeding around the Mediterranean. My impedimenta were reduced to the smallest dimensions, and I took no books, but determined to read carefully the great book which Nature would open before me on the ocean and sky, and also to take note of every incident and object of interest amongst the countries and peoples I should visit. In keeping myself occupied and amused on work of this sort, and carefully abstaining from drugs, I calculated that I should improve my health of body and mind, save myself from brooding on my infirmities, and escape the unhealthiest of all habits—the habit of introspection. By concentrating my thoughts on the world without I would leave no room for phantoms of the world within.

All day long it was my habit to recline on the deck, filling my lungs with the health-laden breeze and my mind with the soothing thoughts inspired by the varying aspects of the ocean and sky ; better medicines than these Science never extracted from the laboratory of Nature. My health improved rapidly and my spirits rose to their normal high level, so that I was soon able to take a keen interest in my surroundings and express my feelings in language which, however high it might soar, fell far beneath them. I started on the principle of seeing everything in the most favourable light, and thereby extracting the utmost value it could afford in the matter of enjoyment both to myself and my readers. I have never observed without pity or disgust those minds that view everything through the medium of their own gloom, which thereby they not only intensify (when it is not a pretence), but impress its discomforts on others who may be unable to see through it.

The last point of British land that I saw was Bardsey Isle, a spot sanctified by the memories of many saints of old, and specially interesting to me, a Cardiffian, as the whilom resting-place of Saint Dyfryg, whose name is associated with Llandaff Cathedral, to which his remains were subsequently transferred.

From Bardsey to Cape Finisterre all was a wilderness of waters horizoned by the sky only. I happen to be one of those lucky individuals who recognise an old friend in what seamen call the " Western Ocean." My spirits rise under its breath, and I never traverse it without renewed delight. On this occasion I was singularly fortunate on renewing my acquaintance with it, for we encountered the after-swell of a south-westerly gale, and were thus enabled to realise the full magnificence of the " Atlantic rollers." They met us like the ranks of a mighty army, countless in their numbers and majestic in their progress, seeming to keep time with a solemn voice that rose and fell in rhythmic cadence like the voice of Eternity crooning the dirge of Time. I watched them day after day with those sensations of

P

awe that one feels in presence of the Infinite and the Unknown, when one's personality vanishes in the vastness of the contemplation.

While at sea I never read, and rather pity those who do ; but if I were obliged to make any author my companion that author should be Homer, and even he would jar on the surroundings unless read in the original, which would harmonise with the music of the sea. When I see people read at sea I cannot help pitying them, for even if their books are not paltry fiction but the sublimest flights of imagination, they are still paltry compared with the great book of Nature unfolded in the sky and ocean. Gibbon has said that he would not exchange his love of books for the wealth of the Indies, and all who enjoy that love will agree with him. But fascinating as it is, when compared with the love of Nature, it is like the love of a beautiful portrait compared with the love of the still more beautiful original.

Tunis was our first port of call, and I renewed my acquaintance with the Near East, begun at Tripoli some years earlier. My stay here lasted about a week, during which I prowled through the streets, explored the wonderful maze of bazaars, and took mental photographs of the natives, both men and women, with which I afterwards amused myself by transferring into words.

On the whole, I had a very pleasant time, and left well-stocked with memories both instructive and amusing, but with my judgment unhypnotised by the glamour of the East. To me that glamour seemed composed of a golden sun in a setting of sapphire, creating an atmosphere that stimulated to sensuous enjoyment while it narcotised intellectual activity. It was augmented by landscapes luxuriating in stately

palms and sombre cypresses, which disposed the
mind to melancholy brooding, so plainly stamped on
the faces of the natives ; and the veiled and muffled
figures of the women, taken in connection with the
barred lattices of their prison-like houses, completed
the spell.

From Tunis we went to Malta, where we stayed
about the same time, but found far less novelty and
variety ; and from Malta to Egypt, landing at
Alexandria, which appeared to me the finest seaport
I had ever seen, with vessels of all sorts and sizes
passing in and out at all hours of the day and night.

I started by rail from thence to Cairo, where I
made a prolonged stay in company with my wife
and her sister ; after which our tour was prolonged
to Cyprus, Beyrut, Latakia, and Sidon.

While at Sidon I was called into a native house
to see a case of enteric fever, for which I prescribed
and gave instructions, *secundem artem*, but which, I
dare say, were never carried out. The incident
reminded me of what a universal demand there is
for medical men. Whenever or wherever one of
them travels he is sure to be requisitioned for some
service, while every other professional man is found
useless and not wanted. I never travelled without
undergoing this experience, and never underwent it
without feeling proud of the unique position my
profession occupies.

Our next port of call was Jaffa, whence I proceeded
to Jerusalem by the light railway, a journey of four
hours. Needless to say, I visited all the holy places,
and the feelings I carried away, from some of them
at least, were feelings of pity that the sublime traditions which they enshrined should be debased with
childish attempts at mere material adornment in their

array of bejewelled pictures and statuettes, myriads of silver lamps and candlesticks of colossal size. On reflection, however, I considered that all this ornamentation deserves respect, inasmuch as it is a concrete expression of those emotions in which mortals assert their birthright to immortality.

My reverence for some of the holy places was rather cruelly tested by the way in which I saw them duplicated. I was shown two sites of Mount Calvary far apart, and neither of them a mount, and I was told there was still a third. In like manner I was shown two Pools of Bethesda, one of them being a piece of waste ground on which rubbish was tipped. I reflected afterwards that this duplication was not a fault but a privilege to the visitor, for it allowed him the benefit of making a choice.

I was at the same time somewhat painfully impressed with the fact that the admirable system of ethics propounded in Jerusalem and preached, if not actually practised, throughout Christendom, should require to be buttressed with myths, marvels, and miracles that, while they win the support of the unthinking multitude, repel the support of a thoughtful minority. No doubt these stories were powerful adjuvants to the spread of Christianity before the dawn of knowledge awoke the spirit of inquiry, but it is just possible that with the extension of this spirit they may prove a weakness rather than a strength. It must, however, be said that their most universal acceptance proves the utility of their purpose, and to remove them prematurely would seem as wicked as removing crutches from those who may not be able to walk without them, but who as soon as they are able to do so will discard them of their own free will.

Jerusalem would seem to me to act on the visitor in two opposite ways. If he is a Christian, burning with the fervour of devotion, he will see confirmation of his faith in every stone of the Holy City, and hear it in every tale he is told and in every prayer recited by his fellow-devotees ; and he will go home with his fanaticism intensified tenfold. But if, on the other hand, he is a hardened sceptic, with a mind trained to weigh evidence and refusing to swallow aught that his reason cannot digest, he will find ample proof for his opinions in all that he sees and hears, and will leave in that frame of mind which theologians charitably call Final Reprobation.

As I studied these two opposites, I felt in the unique position of having a foot in each camp, for while my emotions drew me to the devotees my reason drew me to the sceptics. I, therefore, left the Holy City in the same frame of mind as I entered it, not wiser, but perhaps a little bit sadder, like a man whose admiration for a beautiful fabric is somewhat marred by seeing the insecurity of some of its foundations.

Having called at Algiers, which I would much prefer as a residence to Jerusalem, I returned to Liverpool after a trip that seemed to give me a new lease of life and stored my memory with a world of pictures of infinite variety. In the following winter I again visited Egypt, spending the whole season there, and on my way home visited Athens, a city that fully realised all my expectations. I was charmed with the beauty of its position, the salubrity of its climate, its ruins and associations, and last, but not least, with the urbanity and culture of its inhabitants. Talking to some young ladies who were visitors at the boarding-house where I stopped

I found that they not only spoke English very fluently, but were well read in English literature, even in its most modern phase, as represented by Tennyson, Ruskin, Bernard Shaw, and Oscar Wilde. Indeed, I never met any of our own countrywomen so well acquainted with the two last-named writers.

Here, too, I was witness of a love affair as pretty as any described in the pages of romance. It was so unusual in this prosaic world of ours, and so opposed to our pre-conceived notions of such a character as its hero, that I am tempted to tell it. Its hero belongs to a people who are considered, falsely I believe, to be the last in the world who would allow their hearts to run off with their heads. He was a Jew, and above and beyond even this a German Professor. You would have thought him as impervious to the darts of Cupid as an oyster in its shell.

But even with this double-plated armour the little god was too many for him. He came to Athens to learn Greek colloquially, and the very first day he sat down to dinner in our boarding-house he glanced at the maidservant who placed the soup before him, and then without tasting it or uttering a word suddenly retired to his room. He there summoned our good landlady, rejoicing in the classic name of MacTaggart, hailing from another Athens farther north, and arranged with her to have his meals served privately and that, too, by the same maidservant, who bore the bewitching name of Euphrosyne. This damsel, well-named after one of the Three Graces, waited upon our hero so satisfactorily that he next asked Mrs. MacTaggart if he might engage her to teach him modern Greek. To this the hostess assented on condition that her own daughter should

be present during the lessons.   But instead of receiving instructions from the teacher the pupil began
to make love to her, in a way that one would never
expect from a Jew and a German professor.   She
very discreetly asked what he meant by this conduct,
and he replied that he meant to marry her if she
would have him, and told her mistress that no woman
he had ever met came so near his ideal of Pallas
Athene, an ideal he had always been looking out for.
    Madly in love as he was, this observation was
quite correct.   I never saw a profile more closely
resemble that of the war goddess as stamped on old
Athenian coins.   As he himself was a tall, fine-looking
man on the sunny side of forty, and was not only
a professor, but a possessor of a chateau and estate
in Bavaria, the young lady (who was extremely
intelligent and could converse fairly well both in
French and English, which she had picked up during
her working life, and who, moreover, was an excellent
business woman, able to manage the boarding-house
much better than its owner), saw her chance and
seized it, so they became engaged.
    But the firmament of romantic love with all its
intoxicating brightness never remains cloudless, and
sure enough the clouds gathered in the present case.
The professor's relatives in Bavaria heard of the
engagement and waxed as mad over it as any other
relatives would do under similar circumstances.   In
fact, they badgered him to such an extent that at
last he shrank within his shell, and, cooling down as
suddenly as he had warmed up, he besought his
fiancée to release him from his engagement, promising
that if she did so he would award her a dowry
handsome enough to win her a good husband amongst
her own countrymen.   Euphrosyne on hearing this

rose to the occasion with a spirit that the patron
goddess of old Athens might be proud of.   She
indignantly told him that she had never sought his
love, but that he had forced it upon her.   If he
wanted to back out he was welcome to do so.   She
would not accept an *obolus* of his money, and without
it could get as good a husband as himself.

This speech acted like oil on the suppressed fire
of his passion, and instead of utter extinction caused
it to flare up stronger than ever.   It raised his respect
for Euphrosyne to an unexpected height, and evoking
all the noblest elements in his nature compelled him
to be ashamed of his tergiversation and renew the
engagement more ardently than ever.

He then took her from her situation, bought her
fine dresses, and had her taught music, dancing, and
the various accomplishments and graces befitting a
young lady about to become his wife.   In arranging
for the marriage he met with another obstacle raised
by the demon of religious fanaticism, whose foul
shadow has so often darkened many a fair prospect
of innocent happiness.   The head " josser," as our
seamen call him, of the Greek Church in Athens,
whose technical name is Archimandrite, refused to
permit the marriage unless he renounced the Jewish
religion and became a Christian according to the
Greek ritual.   This must have been a bitter pill to
swallow, but, nevertheless, he did it ; so that every
obstacle to the marriage was now removed, and I
myself in company with our landlady went to the
Archimandrite's house to fix the preliminaries and
arrange the date of the wedding.   It was to take
place in a fortnight, and, sure enough, it then came
off all right.   I, unfortunately, was unable to be
present, having to leave Athens in the meantime,

but I was sent a photo of the happy pair standing hand in hand at the door of their beautiful chateau in Bavaria.

Who after this can say that real life is without romance or that Jew and German are not as human as the rest of us ? No doubt his friends said he had made a fool of himself ; but what generous soul could help admiring his folly, and wishing him and his spouse long and happy lives crowned with the blessings of sons and daughters as spirited and as handsome as themselves ?

I returned from this trip with improved health, a wider outlook, and my taste for travel increased a hundredfold. I had read somewhere that the three most beautiful countries in the world were Jamaica, Java, and Ceylon. The first-named I decided on visiting, as it was the easiest to reach from South Wales, seeing that the Elder Dempster boats went there weekly from the adjacent port of Avonmouth. Having come to this decision I allowed my imagination to run riot in dreams of tropical glory, and was lucky enough to have them realised through the instrumentality of my friend, the Editor of *The Western Mail*, who presented me with a first-class return ticket without binding me to any task-work in return, but merely stipulating that I might, if the spirit moved me, favour him with a few articles dealing with the state of the island. To this I gladly assented, feeling that to do so would be a pleasure rather than a task. Embarking at Avonmouth on the 1st December, 1906, after a pleasant trip of ten days I found myself ashore.

While the reality of Jamaica's beauty, which I have attempted to describe in another work, equalled the picture limned in the glowing colours of my imagination, the reality of its effects upon my health was a grievous disappointment. I lodged in a suburban villa about two miles from Kingston, and went into the city every day, sauntering through it and taking note of every feature and phase of the life that passed before me. The streets, which at first interested me with their novelty, soon became as distressing to traverse as the interminable paths of nightmare. In a country remarkable for the profusion of trees, not a single one stood in those places where trees were most needed, the sun-scorched thoroughfares being as destitute of arboreal shading as the centre of the Sahara, but with layers of dust far more troublesome than the sands of the latter. To walk under a blazing sun between rows of leprosied-looking villas and ramshackle wooden shanties, to meet nothing but clumsy mule carts and groups of ragged and malodorous negroes, varied perhaps with a few whites appearing languid and washed-out, soon became a very monotonous and fatiguing pastime, from which I always returned as limp as a dish-clout. I would then plunge into a large tank of running water, madly forgetting that the momentary refreshment it might afford would entail a heavy penalty later on.

To add to my troubles I had met with no kindred souls with whom I might pass the time pleasantly in congenial chat. Still worse, I was cut off from the companionship of books, and was therefore obliged to fall back on the local newspapers for my intellectual pabulum.

Under such conditions, both mentally and bodily, it was no wonder that my powers of resistance to malarial influence were reduced to zero, and I soon became smitten with a violent fever manifested in a bounding pulse, high temperature, and occasional delirium supervening at night. And just as the passing of a thundercloud seems to leave the sky brighter than before, in like manner when these attacks would pass off my mind became abnormally clear, so that I could take a most accurate survey of my past life and present condition.

I weighed the chances of recovery against those of collapse, and taking into account my age and average state of health I judged that if the former outweighed the latter it was only by a feather's weight. As I had long since disentangled myself from the cob-webs of popular superstition, I looked on the Future without either fear or hope, and on death as the minister of everlasting anæsthesia. While I was thus indifferent about my spiritual prospects I was intensely distressed on reviewing my past life. I found it a comparatively long one, and yet how sterile in results that often make even short lives remembered !

I shuddered to think that in some obscure corner of Kingston's dusty cemetery all my high hopes would lie for ever in a noteless and nameless grave over which no human creature would ever shed a tear. I suppose these gloomy meditations are common to many suffering as I did ; and this leads to the reflection that in counteracting them with its dazzling promises Christianity has done much to atone for the wars, persecutions, massacres, and mental agonies which it has inflicted on mankind from the commencement of the first Crusade till the end of the Thirty Years War.

Like the vast majority of medical men when they are ill, I was sensible enough not to treat myself, but had one of the best doctors in the place called in to do so, and under his care I slowly recovered. As soon as I was able to get up and move around he advised me to leave at once and go to the hills, mentioning as a suitable locality Mandeville, a small market town situated in a lofty and salubrious position about forty miles from Kingston. Acting on this advice I started at once, and by so doing saved my life in a most unforeseen way ; but the experience was shocking in every sense of the word.

A few days after my arrival as I sat writing in the first floor verandah of the hotel at about three o'clock on a delicious afternoon, I was suddenly startled by a strange noise like that which a bursting hurricane might make, and at the same time the house shook and shivered from top to bottom like a ship at the first blow of the hurricane. I instantly diagnosed an earthquake and made for the open with more haste than I thought my legs capable of executing. On getting outside I found that the other inmates of the hotel had preceded me. They stood passively and silently in a group watching the house, and evidently waiting for another shock to demolish it. The negro servants, on the other hand, were in agonies of terror, some on their knees pouring forth incoherent prayers, some standing with outstretched arms and upraised eyes shrieking that the end of the world had come. But whites and blacks were delightfully disappointed, for the world did not come to an end nor did the house come down. Some of its furniture, however, did, and some of its walls were cracked, but beyond this the shock did no material damage.

That night no mail arrived, and we were told that all telegraphic communication had suddenly stopped. This was ominous enough, but worse still, on looking in the direction of Kingston we observed a dull red glare reflected from the sky as if a conflagration were raging below. Next day runners arrived with the news that Kingston had been laid in ruins, amongst which many fires had broken out, completing the devastation which the earthquake began, and all communication by rail and telegraph continued cut off. I was informed that a train would start at six o'clock on the following morning from Williamsfield, six miles from Mandeville, and by this I decided I should go, for I thought I might be able to make myself useful as a medical man, while as a pressman I felt it my duty to go in the interest of the paper I represented.

I started in good time and covered the distance in a buggy while the stars were still shining. There were no passenger carriages, so I had to stand in a goods van, and as the train slowly jolted along I could see evidences of the earthquake multiply. Gangs of black labourers with shovels began to crowd into the vans, also squads of black policemen armed with fixed bayonets, and at every station we passed broken-down buildings increased in number. Still nearer to Kingston I observed gangs of men digging trenches on a hillside, and the significance of their work filled me with horror. When we reached Kingston that horror was increased tenfold.

I met two men driving a dust-cart containing the dead bodies of a man and a woman with their feet projecting behind the cart and the air around them permeated with the strong smell of disinfectant, while the drivers had disinfected mufflers wrapped over their mouths and noses. As I went on I could not identify the streets I had so often traversed, for not a single landmark in the shape of a house was left undemolished.   As the streets of Kingston were very narrow, when the houses of each side fell their roofs met in the centre of the roadway, so that escape seemed impossible to those who were on them. Over these heaps of debris I had to scramble, or make a detour around some of them that were still burning, for the earthquake, as I pointed out, had been succeeded by conflagrations.   Sometimes I encountered iron bedsteads, buckets, and all sorts of utensils indicating where a hardware shop had come to grief, and by its broken bottles I could locate the rum-shop.   It was, however, more usual to find all sorts of commodities mingled in heaps, for most of the shops, or stores, as their owners called them, were universal providers in their own small way and sold a little of everything.

There was one lot which puzzled me a good deal at first.   It was pools of a vitreous-looking substance, bluish grey in colour, slippery to tread, and fatty to touch.   A number of old negro women were digging it up with sticks and putting it into old tins without any interference on the part of the police.   I could not make it out until I searched around and found a brown paper labelled " Sunlight Soap."   Here no doubt a warehouse of that article had fallen and disgorged its contents.

Again, there were other heaps more ominous than any of these.   On passing them nothing was visible but bricks and lumber, but if you were squeamish you would have to hold your nose and you would see swarms of hideous blue flies oscillating around them, and you would probably have to repress a choking sensation.   The objects that lay decomposing under these heaps may be imagined but not described. I saw one poor body lying in the sun.   It had been burned perfectly black and hard—a mere calcinated mass with clothes and flesh inseparable in cinder. By some accident a small patch of white skin had been left on the upper of the right foot, and from this alone one could tell that the body was a white man's.

Farther on lay a body wrapt in a blanket, and yet another on a stretcher carried by two policemen. Going in another direction I met a cart laden with white deal coffins, and by and bye a procession of poor negro women clapping their hands and wailing most pitifully.

There was a fair sprinkling of white men, most of them looking at the heaps of rubbish where their stores once stood. One of them with some assistants was opening a burned cash box on such a heap. The box contained oblong slips of paper like bank notes tied in packets. They had all been burned, but still retained their shapes, although a breath of wind would have sent them flying around in black fragments. The man seemed to think them valuable, for he would not touch them lest he should break them, and he locked the box and took it away with him.

When white men met they invariably shook hands and congratulated each other on being alive. It seemed no matter whether they were friends or enemies or utter strangers to each other, for great grief or great joy makes men forget their petty conventionalities and remember only that they are human. I myself was greeted in this way by men whom I had never met before, but who believed I had been their fellow in the common danger. Of white women I saw none amongst the ruins.

The horrors of the place were intensified by the relentless heat of the sun and the swarms of flies.

I, therefore, made my way with extreme difficulty to
the public garden, where I was told many of the
people were camping out. Here the sights I encountered were even more painful than any I had left,
for the sorrow that one feels in looking at the dead
is tempered by the reflection that their troubles are
over.   No such reflection could temper one's sorrow
at the sight of these living creatures. They were all
poor people, and a great many of them were white.
Some of them had their poor sticks of furniture
around them, including beds and even bedsteads.
Every bed had its wounded occupant, and many
wounded who had no beds were stretched on the
ground, while many others were sitting on chairs in
a semi-conscious or dosing condition.   They had
already been attended by the doctors and nurses,
heads were neatly bandaged, fractured legs and arms
bound in splints—in fact, everything that skill and
humanity could do appeared to have been done for
them.   Their underclothing had not been changed,
and one could often see it spattered with red stains
about the neck and chest.   One poor young woman
with a broken skull was breathing her last. She was
stretched on a bed with the mother and sister bending
over her in a paroxysm of grief.   They were white
people.

The blacks were far more stolid.   Their wounded
lay very quiet, and rarely manifested any suffering
save with a fitful moan.   Amongst the friends who
hovered around them there was little evidence of
emotion, but possibly their perceptions, at all times
blunt, were now dazed and disordered by the awful-
ness of the blow that had so suddenly fallen upon
them.

Under the shade of a great tree some distance

away a large crowd was holding a religious service. I could hear hymn-singing, and from the musical mournful tremor that ran through it I knew that the singers were negroes, and felt that his religion was the only good thing the white man had ever introduced amongst them, for with them, at any rate, it was sincere.

As I had taken my camera with me I had many opportunities of using it, but it struck me that it would not only be callous but irreverent to use a plaything in the presence of so much suffering and sorrow, so I carried it behind my back.

As the day wore on a friend who had travelled with me from Mandeville, and had very considerately brought lunch for both of us, suggested that we should retire somewhere and eat it, so we found a seat in a remote part of the garden and commenced the repast. Every mouthful I took seemed to choke me like hot ashes, hence the mouthfuls I took were very few and the remainder went to the first needy person that passed. I never experienced such a thirst, and would have given gold for a drink of any sort, but none was to be had, not even water. I had also a fearful attack of headache, and felt as if I were booked for another bout of my late illness, so I suggested we should go by the next train to Spanish Town and wait there till our own train should start for Mandeville. I managed to walk, Heaven only knows how, to the remnants of the station, and there I got hauled into a goods van which took me to Spanish Town, reaching Mandeville a little before midnight after an experience of which the remembrance will haunt me like a nightmare during the rest of my life.

This description, which I have been told is the

fullest that reached Great Britain, is the result of notes taken on the spot, and appeared in the *Western Mail* and the Chicago *Daily News*. It was the fullest because for some reason or other the representatives of many leading British newspapers who were in Jamaica as guests of Sir Alfred Jones at the West Indian Agricultural Congress cut down their reports to the very smallest dimensions, as if a cataclysm that caused such havoc were a matter of little interest, in fact not worth talking about. Sir Alfred very generously offered to have my articles published in book form on condition that I should eliminate all reference to the earthquake.

The illness to which I had so nearly fallen a victim turned out to be the means of saving my life, and if I were vain enough to consider myself an object of divine protection I should call my escape providential. Had my health been good I should certainly have continued to lodge in the same house in Kingston. But that house was demolished, a large portion of it being flung on the very bed I slept on, and on which at the hour of the earthquake I should have been taking my siesta after the midday meal. The box containing all my belongings had a similar narrow escape. I had intended leaving it at the shipping-office until my return homeward, in order to save myself the trouble of conveying it around the island, but the landlady persuaded me to leave it at my old lodgings and call for it on my way back. This I did, with the result that I found it safe amongst the ruins, while the shipping-office, where I would have left it, was, with all its contents, burned down. Thus was I doubly fortunate.

My visit to Jamaica did not terminate with the earthquake. I continued to reside at Mandeville, where the salubrity of the climate and the beautiful scenery rapidly restored me to a state of health, which, if not perfect, was at least as good as could be expected.

But if Jamaica left me with many pleasant memories it also robbed me of some pleasing delusions. The chief of these was my belief in the capacity of the Negro to attain the White Man's plane of civilisation, if only given suitable opportunities and environment. Well, here he was for nearly a century placed on the White Man's footing, but without the slightest prospect of equality between them. It would, however, be rash to say that he is therefore the less happy. After long observation one is forced to the conclusion that the most satisfactory modicum of happiness exists amongst the peoples, squalid and semi-savage though they be, who see no standard beyond that already reached, or if they do have no desire of reaching it. First amongst these I would place the Jamaican negroes, who seem to have no ideals, at least in this world, beyond those they have already attained. I indulged in the whimsical fancy that if I were one of them and able to take up the lyre of Omar Khayyam I would thus embody the wishes of my people :

A sturdy helpmate, whether wife or maid,
Able to handle crowbar, pick, and spade,
And earn as much as will support her lord
And thirteen pickaninnies in the shade !

And that the Almighty once a week may stick in
His servant's way some neighbour's finest chicken,
So that on Sunday when from church I come
I may have wherewithal my broth to thicken !

A pint of rum per day to brew my punch,
Yams and salt pork for breakfast, tea, and lunch,
Four walls of wattle and a roof of thatch—
Lo, there be all my wishes in a bunch !

It might well be imagined that my Jamaican experience would have satiated my appetite for travel ;
but that appetite, like my appetite for reading, grew
with what it fed upon, so that I was on the move
again almost before I recovered my breath.   As
ship's surgeon on the " Yeoward Line " I made
three trips to the Canary Islands, but not quite in
succession.   In the same capacity I went on the
" Henderson Line " to South Africa, Ceylon, and
Burmah.   Changing my vocation from surgeon to
journalist I made some very pleasant trips to various
parts of the British Isles, including Edinburgh,
Glasgow, and Dublin, where National exhibitions
had been opened, of which I wrote descriptive
articles.   After this the greatest journey of my life
took place, which included Durban, Colombo, and
Rangoon, and was undertaken in my capacity of
surgeon on board one of the Henderson liners plying
between Glasgow and Rangoon.   I was offered the
position quite unexpectedly, made all my prepara-
tions in two or three hours, and before morning
found myself far down the Bristol Channel.
    It was the first time I had crossed the equator,
and one must cross it when winter reigns in the
southern hemisphere in order to realise the full
strength and grandeur of the Atlantic.   From some
safe point of vantage I used to watch that most
awesome of all scenes when sea and sky are mingled
in a blackness so chaotic that the two seem indis-
tinguishable from each other—a blackness so thick

that it seems suffocating, and is intensified by the sheets of white foam flung round the ship like a winding-sheet woven for her reception by the demons of the deep.

My impressions of Durban were most favourable. I found it a beautiful city, beautifully situated, a resort for health and pleasure that might entitle it to be called the Brighton of South Africa. It seemed a place with a magnificent future, and if I were compelled to live in any part of our Empire outside the British Isles I think I should choose Durban.

Colombo, in Ceylon, was our next destination, and I found the chief interest centre in its inhabitants, who impressed me more as a picturesque than a powerful lot. Both sexes of the upper and middle classes were dressed almost alike in brilliantly-coloured petticoats, embroidered jackets, and elaborate coiffures, so that it was difficult for a stranger to diagnose which was which. This difficulty was still further increased by the smooth, beardless faces, slender limbs, and air of effeminacy common to both.

They impressed me as being a people easy to subdue and easy to hold in subjection, and yet their history hardly justifies this impression.

I left Ceylon with regret, for its climate suited my health, its scenery was beautiful, and its natives very interesting, while its British residents were most hospitable and friendly, as indeed they are in all our tropical possessions. At Rangoon I found different climatic conditions which rendered my visit far from pleasant. It was the wet season, and the atmosphere was muggy and depressing, which compelled me to spend most of my time stretched on a couch in my hotel, where I managed to keep body and soul together with doses of quinine and whiskey.

I generally deferred my walks till the afternoon, when the meridian heat had abated, and then I would stroll through all parts of the city taking mental photographs of the place and the people.

It is here above all the places I have ever seen that all the racial types of the East and the West in all their diversity of costume and manner meet in the hustle and bustle of competition in pushing their wares on the market. Of all these competitors the Chinese appeared to me to be the most succesful and the most likely to survive in the struggle for existence. Their well-developed physique, their capacity for accommodating themselves to all sorts of circumstances, their wonderful fecundity, industry, trustworthiness, and thrift, mark them out for a paramount position in the future of Burma.

I was more overjoyed to leave Rangoon than any other place I ever visited. I felt that if I had remained there another month I should remain till Michael sounded the *reveille*. And yet one of the city officials who came on board quite surprised me by his stalwart frame and look of robust health, and I was still more surprised when he informed me that during a residence of eighteen years he never had an hour's illness ; and the secret of the miracle was that throughout all that period he never once went to bed sober. But then he was a Scotsman.

My latest journey was my third to the Canaries, as ship's surgeon, and occurred in the first year of the Great War.

Though the War while it lasts has put an end to my travelling, it has not put an end to my hope of doing so as soon as the opportunity offers. But if the opportunity does not come soon, my declining strength warns me it will come too late, and I must be content to remain at home till I reach the bottom of the hill.

And this reminds me that the course of a normal life is like a journey that leads over a hill. In the first half, which comprises youth and manhood, we travel slowly to reach the top, and with the approach of age we commence the descent, when the pace is wonderfully quickened, so that we seem to pass the milestones as an express train passes the telegraph poles, and we find ourselves at the bottom before we know where we are.

To me this descent is not such a mournful prospect as it may seem to the onlooker. In looking over my struggles of the past through the mists of Memory, that minimise rather than magnify, I seem like an old campaigner who, debarred from active warfare, still finds quiet enjoyment in the mental survey of those battlefields where he won victory or suffered defeat. What contributes in an almost equal degree to happiness is the privilege of living in the most stupendous epoch of the world's history : when the war of Right against Might, of Light against Darkness, absorbs the energies of civilised mankind. But even if this war did not exist to brighten my evening sky with the promise of a brilliant to-morrow, I have other sources of happiness available against the morbid broodings which some- times gather around the evening of Life, like clouds round the setting sun. I have many friends on whose moral and material influence I could rely if ever Fortune compelled me to seek such help. In their society I lay aside the burden of age and give free rein to my fancy in the region of literature or exercise my judgment in political discussion, where the very oldest of us feel as infallible as the very youngest. Or, again, in listening to Nature's sweetest music—the prattle of my grandchildren—I am transported back to the happy days of childhood, which I can imagine but have never experienced.

By means of these associations and surroundings, which compose the Indian summer of my life, I find my old age happier than any previous stage of my existence. I am quite sure it might have been otherwise if I had been cradled in the lap of luxury, and thereby prevented from comparing the sweet and the bitter draughts with which Fortune alternately fills her goblet. Remembrance is, as it were, a dark background on which subsequent pictures are projected with all their bright colours intensified by the contrast.

Human life might be compared to a day, inasmuch as it consists of three stages—youth, manhood, and old age—corresponding to morning, noon, and evening. Each of these stages has its own peculiar charm, but not one of them concentrates in itself the charms of all. Youth, like the morning, has its freshness, manhood its fervour, and old age its serenity.

Youth and manhood have their sorrows as well as old age, and feel them quite as keenly. Even childhood's happy days, of which we hear so much, have their sorrows, and if these sorrows are less deep and abiding than the sorrows of old age they are far more numerous. The pleasures of youth and manhood are the pleasures of the senses, and their intoxication is often followed by unpleasant reaction. The pleasures of old age are the pleasures of the intellect and affections, pleasures that soothe and sweeten and beget no regrets.

Somebody has said that old age is a disappointment ; but if that is so it is because youth and manhood have not been used to the best advantage.

I myself, now standing on an eminence of three score and eleven years, survey the long vista of my past life stretching away to the remote horizon when my pilgrimage began on a stretch of desert that seemed interminable, threatening, as it were, to swallow my whole life in the journey across. Interminable as it seemed then, from my present standpoint it seems only a dark spot on the brim of the horizon, from which I was transported into the intervening region by means of the magic which kindly Nature had given me in the love of Books. As I look over this region I find it diversified with hills and valleys and beautiful landscapes laid out in picturesque variety, abounding in crops of fruits and flowers, made melodious with the songs of innumerable birds, and peopled with the wise and good of all countries and of all ages.

This retrospect as seen from my eminence of seventy-one years covers the region I should again traverse if I were born anew and had my choice of all the pathways open to the life of Man. And the best guidance that I found in it is acknowledged in the following lines addressed to My Books on my sixty-fifth birthday. They strike the keynote of my Life :

Companions of my youth and age,
    To you a grateful verse is due,
For searching over memory's page
    I find no faster friends than you.

They that to me are all in all
    Year after year keep fewer growing ;
And woe is me to see them fall
    Beneath the bony scytheman's mowing.

The farther down the hill I go
   The loss of each I keener feel,
And recognise in every blow
   A wound that time can never heal.

But you, my books, exalted high
   Beyond the range of lethal dart!
Can with a constant light supply
   The darkened chambers of the heart.

In your companionship I share
   Delight unfailing, of a kind
That mocks the means of millionaire,
   And leaves no bitter taste behind.

Bless you, my ever-constant friends,
   That change not with the changing wind;
Your ready sympathy attends
   On every mood that moves the mind.

What tho' we differ now and then,
   Our well-tried friendship never fails—
Alas, amongst my fellow-men
   How oft another rule prevails!

To you as costly, quaint, or rare,
   A blind belief I do not pin,
But place my first and foremost care
   On what your covers keep within.

Nor do I on your covers dote
   With mind in reverential frame,
For friendship in a modest coat
   To me is friendship all the same.

But none the less I do opine
  That texture strong and fair device-
Should mark the caskets that enshrine
  My chosen gems of peerless price.

Around your ranks in order rang'd
  The while my loving eyes are cast,
I think how all the world has chang'd
  And we the same from first to last.

Ah, well-a-day, while yet a boy
  Chain'd to the oar in adverse tide !
You were my compensating joy,
  And fortune promised none beside.

But by your aid the fickle jade
  Was forc'd to play another tune,
When wind and wave their favours gave
  And sped me on through manhood's noon

And now towards the quiet West
  While fast the sun unclouded moves,
I sigh for nothing unpossesst ;
  Your influence all sufficient proves.

When gain and loss are reckoned o'er—
  " O Life," a not ungrateful debtor,
I'll say, " You might have given more,
  But could have given nothing better."